# ECONOMIC OFFENCES

# ECONOMIC OFFENCES

A COMPENDIUM
OF CRIMES
IN PROSE
AND VERSE

## S. SUBRAMANIAN

OXFORD
UNIVERSITY PRESS

# OXFORD
UNIVERSITY PRESS

Oxford University Press is a department of the University of Oxford.
It furthers the University's objective of excellence in research, scholarship,
and education by publishing worldwide. Oxford is a registered trademark of
Oxford University Press in the UK and in certain other countries

Published in India by
Oxford University Press
YMCA Library Building, 1 Jai Singh Road, New Delhi 110 001, India

ISBN-13: 978-0-19-809032-8
ISBN-10: 0-19-809032-3

Typeset in Goudy Old Style 14/18
by Le Studio Graphique, Gurgaon 122 001

This little collection of
pieces is dedicated,
with love and gratitude,
to the memory of
RAVI JOHN MATTHAI,
one of very few men
of whom it can be said
that they were God's own

# Contents

*Heroes of Our Times*

## VERSE FOLLIES
### The Lyrical Sides to
### Economy and Society

# Acknowledgements

Of the twenty-two pieces featured in this volume, sixteen have appeared in print earlier, in their present or in slightly different forms. The precise citations are provided in the relevant chapters. Here, I would like to thank the Editor, Dr Siddharth Varadarajan, of *The Hindu*, for permission to reproduce Chapters 1, 2, 3, 4, 5, 6, 9, 10, 12, and 22 from various issues of the newspaper's Sunday Magazine over the years 2000 and 2001. Chapter 15 is an enhanced and revised version of a piece titled '1936 and All That' which appeared in the January 2010 issue of the Royal Economic Society's *Newsletter*, while Chapter 17 ('Clerihews in Merry Hues ...') appeared in the July 2009 issue. For permission to reprint these chapters, thanks are owed to the Editor, Professor Peter Howells, of the *Newsletter of the Royal Economic Society*. I acknowledge, with thanks, the Publisher, M.E. Sharpe of *Challenge: The Magazine of Economic Affairs* for permission to reproduce

Chapter 16 ('An Ode on Poverty: The Saga of World Poverty') which originally appeared in the July/August 2009 issue of the magazine. Finally, I am grateful to the Editors, Dr Tae-Hee Jo and Dr Ted P. Schmidt, of *The Heterodox Economics Newsletter*, for permission to reprint Chapters 18 ('Concavity: The Pivotal Point') and 19 ('Alcoholic Disclaimer') which were originally published, under the joint title of 'Verse and Worst: Two Poetic Excesses in Economics or, perhaps, Two Economic Excesses in Poetry', in the 30 June 2010 issue of the *Newsletter*.

# Apologia, viz. Sorry!

A major part of this 'book'—such as it is—was written over the years 2000-1. Many of the pieces (specifically, parts or versions of Chapters 1, 2, 3, 4, 5, 6, 9, 10, 12, and 22) appeared in *The Hindu*'s Sunday Magazine, and I am grateful to the newspaper's publisher and its editor for permission to reproduce them here. I cannot recall that there was any conscious design driving the production of the pieces. It is almost as if they wrote themselves, over a period which witnessed a dismaying degeneration in the social and political life of India and the world around. I belong to a generation that came a little after Midnight's Children—but only a little after. People like me are too old not to feel an almost embittered frustration over the gradual dissolution of their youthful dreams for India.

That sentiment is as truthful as it is self-indulgent. I suppose I was looking for some un-pompous mechanism to cope with this very pompous affliction, and such a mechanism, in the event, was afforded by the literature of my childhood. The real or imagined innocence of childhood's distant past served as a soothing contrast to the very real villainies of the present. It also served as a curmudgeonly medium for ventilating numerous ill-tempered dissatisfactions with the world around, but without having to adopt a grim-death view of the matter.

A decade, in some ways, is a long period of time, and many of the pieces in this collection are likely to appear dated today: some are set in a time that was a bleak period for the prospects of secularism in this country, while others refer to specific events such as constitutional review, match-fixing in cricket, and unsavory armament deals, which are now memories of things past (though they have a way of reappearing in new incarnations as things present). It might help to know that several years ago I had sent an earlier, somewhat different, and definitely unexplained version of this manuscript to a prominent Indian publishing house, where it languished in the children's section for months before it was pronounced unsuitable for tender minds. I have not done much with the manuscript in the years since then, save to delete a few pieces and add a few more, before venturing publication again, now. This time I have taken care to include an explanatory preface. I hope it softens the blow apart from assisting with locating the book in its proper time (though I also happen to believe that any time is a proper time for dealing with certain intimately national phenomena such as caste and corruption).

In David Lodge's book, *Therapy* (1995), a near Eastern character called Nizar '... speaks immaculate English, but I think he must have read a lot of P.G. Wodehouse once.' Nizar is a man after my own heart—and the hearts, I daresay, of more Indians than persons of any other nationality. In many ways, it seems natural for an Indian of a certain age, social origin, and profession (the impossibly depressing one, in my own case, of an academic economist) to hark back to Wodehouse as a literary means—admittedly not avant-garde—of coming to terms with India's contemporary problems. The irony involved in this would be a subject worthy of serious analysis as an aspect of the Postcolonial Condition, if it were not as comical as it is.

And it is not only Wodehouse. This book is haunted by the ghosts of several men who, I suspect, would be more readily recognized in this country than in the countries of their origin—Stephen Leacock, Robert Benchley, Donald Ogden Stewart, Ogden Nash, A.P. Herbert, D.B. Wyndham Lewis, Arthur Marshall, J.B. Morton ('Beachcomber'),

Ronald Searle, W.G. Sellar and R.J. Yeatman, and Geoffrey Willans. Indeed, there are some gags in the ensuing pieces which are due to one or the other of these gentlemen, only I cannot remember which—for instance, 'what with daddy's face becoming darker by the day (and virtually invisible by night)' (Benchley?); 'with a Welsh grandmother on one side and an orang-outang on the other' (Leacock?); and Heaven knows what else, as a consequence of such thorough internalization as to defy precise recall.

The notion of the Fuzzy Thinker invoked from time to time in this book, I owe entirely to the economist Dudley G. Luckett, who published an incredibly funny article titled 'The Inverted Tetrahexahedron' in, as it happens, a deadly serious professional journal.* The Dismal Science does, it seems, throw up the odd humorist. Why, Leacock himself taught political economy at McGill University!

It remains to record the shocking fact that there are a number of people who have to take some responsibility for this work. If I should miss out, through oversight, on acknowledging some of the many individuals that have offered comments, suggestions, encouragement,

---

* Dudley G. Luckett, 1971, 'The Inverted Tetrahexahedron: A Personal Account of How the ICBM was Discovered', *Journal of Political Economy*, 79(4): 933–7.

and instigation, I have no doubt they shall regard this as cause for immense gratitude to me for my forgetfulness. The less fortunate beings are Alaka Basu, Kaushik Basu, Sukanta Chaudhary, Aloke Roy Chowdhury, Barbara Harriss-White, Kavita Iyengar, Mozaffar Qizilbash, Suguna Ramanathan, Mike Redley, Anita Roy, Shiva Shankar, Usha Shankar, Paul Seabright, Sanjay Subrahmanyam, Kaushik Sunder Rajan, Rajeswari Sunder Rajan, and Adam Swallow.

As always, my greatest debt is to my wife, Prabha Appasamy, for rescuing me repeatedly with unpopular, quietly insistent, and unfailingly on-target criticism, while never abandoning hope for this hopeless book.

May 2013                                    S. Subramanian

# Preface

A preface, children, is where I get to tell you what this book is about, and why it's such a super book, and how you should use it, and why it's such a super book, and the sorts of ways in which it will help you, and why it's such a super book, and when is the best time for you to touch your Mummies and Daddies for the modest sum you'll need to buy one copy for yourself and another for your worst enemy and a third for the road, and why it's such a super book. But Uncle S (that's me, slowpokes) loves you far too much, and is far too little infected by the vulgar commercial instincts of his times, to want to resort to any such blatantly offensive, not to say unethical, self-advertisement, except insofar as to suggest, gently, for your favourable consideration, the passing thought that if you were to buy this book, you should be doing no more than satisfying the Pigou-Dalton principle of transfers, seeing that you're a bunch of overweight brats with well-heeled parents, in sharp contradistinction to an underpaid Fuzzy Thinker burdened by an unspeakably tragic sense of his own impecuniousness (that's me, again, dunderheads). It is my earnest hope that you've got the point.

Setting aside this sordid pecuniary theme (assuming you've bought your three copies each), let us return to it, for it is, after all, the presiding theme of the times in which you are growing up, which is all about describing that ineffably wondrous trajectory from unprincipled moppethood to unprincipled adulthood, or what one might, in an unguarded moment of poetic sentiment, refer to as the parabola of hoodlumhood.* These are fraught times to live through, with so much pressure on you to succeed, as you will recall from your hourly experience of Mummy's hysterical promise to throttle, first, you, and, then, herself, because of her inability to live down the tragedy of the news that one of your cousins has already passed the SAT exam; a second has crammed everything on offer from three separate tutorial coaching centres; and a third one's father is fully prepared to bribe his son's way through engineering college. And where does that leave you, you abysmal, uncaring, shameless, inconsiderate blot

---

* The sort of thing one may expect from P.G. Wodehouse's poet Ralston McTodd, who is credited with the immortal phrase 'Across the pale parabola of Joy ...'

on the family? Your environment, you poor dears, is saturated to bursting with overwhelming threats and apparently unattainable opportunities: caste, pseudo-secularism, minorityism, (other people's) poverty, tradition, modernity, postcoloniality, liberalization, corruption, competition, nationalism, and NRIism ... What will you ever do, you defenceless little things?

It's obvious that you need help, desperately. And who better to provide it than Uncle S?

Hence these stories, conceived and written with the greatest care in the world, and with just one end in view: that you may acquire, through a proper cultivation of your minds and souls, that unique combination of intelligence and morality which alone will enable you to comprehend, to cope, to overcome, and eventually to succeed.

It's value for money, dammit. Buy four, get one free. (Daddy's purse, as you know, is cunningly tucked away between the pillows.)

Your Dear Old Uncle S

All the pieces by their subject-matter make a direct appeal, are vigorous in their expression, and in their moral tone tend to exalt the best instincts of human creatures.

—S.E. Winbolt
(Preface to *English Poetry for the Young*, p. 1, Blackie and Son Limited, London, 1904)

# PROSE FOLLIES
## Understanding Economics
### A Child's Guide to Some Major Themes

Schopenhauer maintained that life is a perpetual oscillation between ennui and suffering. If he had said 'economics' for 'life', he could not have hit the nail squarer on the head. Not the least reason for the dismalness of the Dismal Science is the boredom it succeeds in broadcasting. Young people who are put off by the discipline tend to grow into adults who are put off by the discipline. The accompanying pieces, written in the style of well-worn classics of literature for children, or of instructional tales for juveniles, are intended as a helpful medium for getting younger persons interested in the subject (and in some of its near relatives, such as law, sociology, politics, and international relations). A special effort has been made to embed the pieces in a setting reflecting contemporary manners and mores. They may, of course, also be read by adults (preferably under expert supervision).

## Family Life

In stories that are truthfully imagined, and choicely told, we may see family life, the tenderness of parentage, the sweetness of childhood, the pleasant claims of kinship, the faithfulness of true friendship, the romance of love, and the firm bond of duty.

—Arthur Mee
(*The Children's Encyclopaedia*,
Volume I, p. 110, The Educational
Book Company Limited, London)

# 1

## Globalization

### A Story from the Indian Diaspora*

This is an extremely short and poignant story, and goes as follows.

*This piece originally appeared, under the same title, in *The Hindu*'s Sunday Magazine of 30 September 2000.

Once upon a time, just the other day, a baby girl was born to a couple. The father, upon finishing school in Chennai, had taken the SAT exam and gone on to the United States of America to graduate, postgraduate, doctorate, and post-doctorate in software programming, exactly as the mother had done, the two having become engaged to each other at birth through an understanding between their respective sets of parents, the idea being that together they would make as many dollars in California in as little time as possible, this being the right thing to do for all good families. Mummy and Daddy, who were very keen on ethnic identity and national culture, which was also the rule among all good families, scoured the IndianHeritagedotcom websites on the Internet in order to find for their newborn baby a properly Sanskritic name that could be properly anglicized in a stylish contraction. After much effort they lovingly settled on Aishmita, which, as a mathematician would put it, is a convex combination of the names of two National Goddesses of Bollywood. At home and at school, little Aishmita came to be called Ata. (This, of course, had nothing to do with her pale, pudgy, floury complexion.)

Mummy and Daddy loved little Ata dearly, but they didn't have an awful lot of time for her, seeing as how they were so tirelessly preoccupied with discovering their national identity, making lots of transnational money, helping to build a temple in San Jose, and assisting with raising dollars to demolish a place of religious worship belonging to another community back home in India. So they got their old widowered grandfather, Thatha, to come and live with them and look after Ata. Now Thatha was barely functionally literate, having had some sort of education with an accent on solid geometry and hydrostatics, which had equipped him to retire as a high functionary in the Department of Posts and Telegraphs, but otherwise left him utterly incapacitated when it came, for example, to making anything of television advertisements. The consequence of all of this was calamitous, as we shall immediately see.

In his muddled and fuzzy way, Thatha was hopeless when it came to dealing with the consumer products of an advanced industrialized economy. This was too bad in an era of globalization. In the cause of little Ata's personal hygiene, what do you think he went and did? Why, he brushed her teeth with hair-dye and washed her hair with a bleacher. The outcome is there for you to see in the accompanying pictures (being self-portraits, they were drawn by Ata herself who, as you can see, allowing for some smudging, was a gifted child and, like other diasporadic children, attended a special school): little Ata acquired shiny black teeth and sparkling white hair. Mummy and Daddy flew into a rage. They diced up Thatha into little bits in the shredder and concealed the outcome(s) in the refrigerator. This is why this is a true, but chilling, story.

Children, there are at least two lessons to be learnt from all of this. First, Mummy and Daddy were perhaps too quick to denounce the heterodox sage Amartya Muni as an agent of the missions of the other community; things may yet not have come to quite this pass if they had heeded his advice on the importance of literacy. What's the use of gobalization if you can't tell hair-dye from a bleacher? Second, any one of you could try and transform this skimpy outline of a theme into a 400-page novel. Don't be

disappointed if you should get the Crooker Prize, even if you're right in believing you deserved the Crookest.

# 2
## The Economics of Crime

### Naughty Ata*

This is a story of juvenile crime, from the dreadful conclusion of which, I hope, all young children aspiring to be useful, self-reliant citizens will learn something of value. It goes as follows.

* This piece originally appeared, under the same title, in *The Hindu*'s Sunday Magazine of 19 November 2000.

Ata was a sweet little nine-year-old and cousin of the Ata whom we have encountered in an earlier tale of terrible truth. (Tales of terrible truth ran in the family.) While that Ata lived in San Jose, this one lived in Chennai. Just like the other Ata, this one too was precocious and prodigious and wholly unbearable and the apple of her ambitious Mummy's eye. Mummy always wanted the best for little Ata, and so made sure she always came first in class (having earlier run her car over Ata's annoying scholastic rival, in a hit-and-run near the school gates). Wanting the best for Ata also meant that Ata learnt *Bharatanatyam* and ballet, Carnatic music and the piano, swimming and computer software, and rapid reading and creative writing. Mummy kept an especially close watch on Ata's reading, making sure she was fed with a steady diet of that on which she (Mummy) herself had grown up (in a loose manner of speaking, of course)—to wit, the complete works of the well-known children's writer Aenid Blighter.

At the time this story opens, Mummy was having trouble with Ata's persistent demands for money: in her girlish, innocent way, Ata was forever strapped for the ready, needing, as she did, money for tuition, money for dresses, money for a day out with the girls, money for email and internet chatting, money for a little usurious lending on the side... Mummy was very sensitive and indulgent, but she had to draw the line *somewhere* (what with Daddy's face becoming darker by the day [and virtually invisible by night]), and she decided she would draw it at Ata's requisition for two thousand rupees towards a pair of Knifee Shoes. All the tantrums and wheedling in little Ata's considerable repertoire were of no avail: Mummy stood firm. Ata realized she had no option now but to employ some wily stratagem. She knew she had to get her mother in a nice, soft, pliable frame of mind, so that the touch, when effected at the opportune moment, would bear fruit. What better than to fill the maternal bosom with pride by doing a spot of creative writing, and that too in the style of Mummy's own favourite author? With this in mind, Ata sat herself in front of the computer, and wrote a story which she cannily dedicated to 'the bestest Mummy in the whole world'. Here's the story (which, I hope you'll remember, is a story within a story).

### Marjorie's First Term at Mushingham Manor

The train rounded the corner and Marjorie, her heart fluttering as she sought to catch her first glimpse of Mushingham Manor, caught her first glimpse of Mushingham Manor. Mushingham Manor was hideous. (Marjorie's heart was still fluttering.) Mushingham Manor had four-and-a-half towers—

North Tower, South Tower, East Tower, West Tower and North-East Tower, which was a bit moth-eaten. Meanwhile somebody tried to push Marjorie out of the train, but Marjorie held on to the hand-rail in time. It was Elsa, the most spiteful girl in class, whom everybody hated and who hated everybody, that had tried to push Marjorie out. On Marjorie's first night in Mushingham Manor, the spiteful Elsa spitefully drenched her with cold water from a decanter. Marjorie was a fierce, high-spirited girl (with a Welsh grandmother on one side and an orang-outang on the other), and she broke the decanter over Elsa's head. Elsa wept and howled, and it transpired she was spiteful because life at home with her cruel stepmother was miserable, and the kind-hearted girls of the Upper First Dorm all wept and howled with Elsa, until Miss Starchit came in and knocked them all soundly on the head, and everybody kissed each other wetly and became friends and went to sleep happily. The next day the girls had a deal of fun ragging Mam'zelle, the French Mistress. The following night, after lights-out, the girls had a Secret Dip in the swimming pool, at which a couple of the less experienced swimmers drowned. The night following, they had a thrilling Midnight Feast, at which again two girls died of rat-poisoning. Each day was more exciting than the previous one until at last the final day of the First Term dawned. It was the day of the lacrosse match between Mushingham Manor and St Elba's. Marjorie played hard but fair—until a girl from the opposition tried to trip her. At that, Marjorie said both 'Gosh!' and 'Golly!' to herself. She knew desperate measures were called for now, for the honour of her school was at stake. Heaving and pushing and scratching and biting, she scored eleven goals—one goal for each St Elban she sent to hospital. When the whistle blew, Mushingham Manor had won by a margin of one goal! Hurrah for Mushingham Manor! The match was followed by tea. What a scrumptious treat was in store for the hungry, strapping girls! Muffins and hot buttered scones and cucumber sandwiches and jam tarts and rich, creamy chocolate cake and pints and pints of lemonade! Marjorie did well for herself. After tea Marjorie was sick. This brings us to the end of Marjorie's first term at Mushingham Manor.

The story seemed to be having the desired effect. Mummy's eyes were pricking with happy tears. What a clever, talented child she had! With this kind of beginning, she should be good for at least a Commonwealth before she was quite out of her teens! Mummy seemed to be in a spell. Ata calculated that this, if ever, was the right moment for another touch. She sprang it on Mummy. Horror of horrors!

For all that Mummy seemed to be in the land of Far Away and Long Ago, she was still firmly attached to her purse strings. Do you think she relented? Guess again. Almost mechanically, she said *no*.

Ata had had enough. While Mummy was still in a trance, she busied herself with a pail of water and a water heater, and various computer terminals which she hooked on to this and that, while hooking this and that on to the computer terminals and a clutch of live wires on to Mummy. Little Ata knew all about electrodes and positive and negative charges and good conductors and voltage, and ignorant as I am of these matters, I can't tell you precisely how she did it, but before you could say 'Faraday', she was electrocuting Mummy. While Mummy was frying nicely to a frazzle, Ata rifled Mummy's purse and made off (with two thousand rupees firmly clutched in her little sweaty fingers) on twinkling toes to the shoe shop. We seem all set for a happy ending, but hold on—here comes the terrible part of the tale.

By the time Ata arrived at the shoe shop, excess demand had overtaken her, and the Knifee Shoes she so dearly desired were clearing the market at two thousand and five hundred rupees. Too late, oh too late! I trust you've learnt the moral of this terrible tale. No, no, it's not a story of crime and punishment; it's one of crime and inadequate reward. In order to get the best out of crime, it's imperative at all times to be in tune with market intelligence. Is it too much to hope that you've now understood the true meaning of all those long and hard words you're always hearing these days, words like globalization, liberalization, marketization, privatization and the gains from trade? The lesson of, and for our times, children, is this: crime does pay, but not nearly enough unless you learn to play the market right.

# 3

## The Competitive Economy
### Fata's Fate*

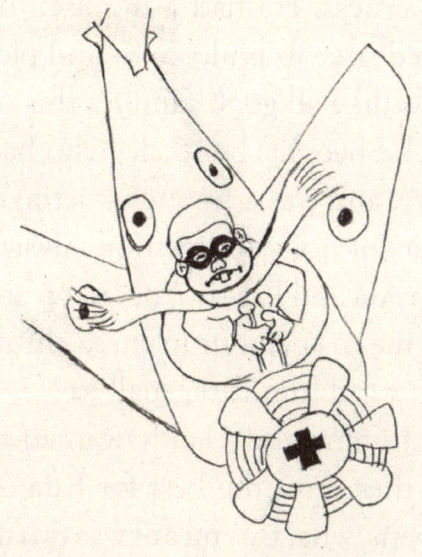

This story is about a brother of little Ata's, whom we encountered in the previous tale. This brother was a couple of years older than Ata, and while

* This piece originally appeared, under the same title, in *The Hindu*'s Sunday Magazine of 10 December 2000.

Mummy and Daddy loved him every bit as much as they did Ata (which was a whole lot), one should be pardoned for sometimes believing that there's no accounting for tastes. For if you saw the little fellow (and assuming you weren't his parents or a saint), you would acquire an intimate understanding of why Lewis Carroll called all boys toads. The little chap was both overweight and pudgy, and worse still, had an egregious charm rendered the more unbearable by his obvious cleverness. He had a despised unemployed uncle with a degree in philosophy and plenty of time on his hands (like all good families this one too had its own Black Sheep). The uncle, who had a passion for symmetry, and was a frequent victim of the boy's chronic bouts of noisy indigestion, always called the two children Ata and Far—no, no, not a naughty word will you get me to spell out in these chronicles! Well then, let's just call him Fata, shall we?

Just as Mummy and Daddy wanted the best for Ata, so did they want the best for Fata. At the time this story opens, what this meant was two things. First, Fata had to win a Junior Science Talent Scholarship; second, he had to win the first prize in a short story competition organized by *The Hindu's Young World* publication. In the cause of the first goal, Fata was required, for his own good, to sway back and forth nightly, while reciting (for if he had a weakness, it was astronomy): 'The sun is a red ball of fire. The sun is a red ball of fire. The sun ...' Mummy and Daddy were committed parents, and they kept the vigil with Fata. Every time Fata lapsed, Daddy was to hand with a well-directed cuff, and if Daddy should occasionally doze off, Mummy was always there to administer her sharp little pinches.

As far as the second goal was concerned, Thatha had already taken care of it: in order that Fata may grow up to be a manly little fellow, Thatha had fed the boy tirelessly with the books of Captain W.E. Jaunts. With all that literature sloshing around inside his system, it was a simple enough matter for Fata to turn out the following story of high adventure:

## Caught in a Dogfight

Squadron-Leader James Squigglesworth whistled tunelessly to himself as he steered his Spitfire homeward. It had been a bad show. They had been caught in a hail of tracer bullets and enemy ack-ack. He was relieved to see that Binger and Calgy had bailed out before their craft went up in flames. But two other companions hadn't been so fortunate, and went west. Tomorrow, Squiggles told himself with a grim smile, they would be back with reinforcements, and teach the Hun a thing or two. Suddenly he stiffened. From out of nowhere, as it seemed, three

Heinkels were bearing down on him, screaming in unison with their engines at full throttle. Squiggles' normally placid blue eyes contracted to slits, until all you could see was a pair of steely, menacing points of gimlet. His grim face became grimmer, his mirthless smile mirthlesser, and his square jaw rectangular, as he suddenly went into a Himmelmann turn, throwing in, for good measure, a Zimmermann turn and a Heinemann turn as well. Two of the Heinkels, which were converging on Squiggles from his flanks, had no time to react. Thrown off guard, they had no means of recovering, and set as they were on a collision course, they crashed into each other. 'Two Jerries down and one to go', muttered Squiggles to himself. He steadied himself as he came out of his tail-spin, and made straight for the third Heinkel. Unwaveringly, and with nerves of steel, he framed the enemy's cockpit on his cross-hairs and pressed the trigger. Nothing happened. He pressed again. Still nothing happened. 'Blast!' ejaculated Squiggles. He had run out of ammo! There was only one thing for it, now. Even as he came under a storm of tracers, he unflinchingly picked up his petrol can, took careful aim, and flung it with all his strength at the enemy's fuselage. The petrol can found its target! He heard a deafening roar as the fuselage erupted, and could feel the flames singeing his hair, as he careened out of the way of the plummeting wreckage, just in time. The last thing he saw was the pilot ejecting, and as the parachute billowed open he caught a glimpse of a face contorted with fury and hatred. It was Erich von Schtrongmein! 'Strewth!' muttered Squiggles to himself, as he made for British lines.

That night Fata went to sleep muttering to himself: 'The sun is a red ball of fire. Strewth!' The following morning, his classmate Navyudh dropped in at Fata's, and offered to mail Fata's short story for him on his way back home. Fata, who had no intention of waddling up to the post office if he could help it, agreed readily enough. Navyudh helpfully mailed the story, but before doing so (and casting a quick look all round), he erased Fata's name from the manuscript in a business-like way and inserted his own in place. That afternoon was the afternoon of the Junior Science Talent Exam. As was their custom, Fata and Navyudh met a few minutes before school at the bushes in the corner, for their daily fag. On this occasion, Navyudh also extracted a small flask he had secreted into his pocket, and let Fata have a long draught of his (Navyudh's) father's smuggled whisky. Poor Fata became thoroughly disorientated. At the exam, he wrote: 'The red is a ball fire of sun.' Naturally, he didn't get the Science Talent Scholarship. As for the short story, it was judged the best in the competition, but for reasons we have already seen, it was Navyudh that got the prize, a fact that couldn't be changed even though Fata's Mummy nearly gouged out Navyudh's Mummy's eye, and Fata's Daddy peached on Navyudh's Daddy to the Enforcement Directorate.

As you can imagine, Fata was traumatized. Indeed, he was scarred for life. By Mummy and Daddy. 'Here', said Mummy, 'is a red ____' '____ ball fire of sun', completed Daddy, as, wielding, respectively, the seasoning ladle and the electric iron, they proceeded to brand their loudly squealing offspring on his ample nether quarters (or halves, rather, if you wish to get the notion of hemispheres right). It's such a sad and terrible tale, children. Won't you ever learn, even if your parents are beyond all instruction?

Here's the simple moral of this dreadful story. Children, please, please stop being competitive. Start, instead, being monopolistic. Like Navyudh, learn to eliminate all competition. The easiest way to do that may well be to eliminate all competitors. There's a nice economist uncle called Kaushik Basu, who has written a book on Industrial Organization which you should all read, and in which, I shouldn't be surprised to discover, it has been proved that entry deterrence is a sub-game perfect equilibrium.

## The Way of the Little Scholar

What shall we say then, when the question
before us is that of *educating children*?

—Maria Montessori
(*The Montessori Method*,
translated by Anna E. George, p. 20,
William Heinermann, London, 1920)

# 4
## Human Capital
### Ta-Ta's Test*

This terrible tale is about a terrible aspect of social injustice, called caste discrimination, which has become such a shameful feature of our country's history, thanks to the doings of two nasty old men called B.P. Mandal and V.P. Singh. We shall, in what

* This piece originally appeared, under the same title, in *The Hindu*'s Sunday Magazine of 31 December 2000.

follows, tell the sad and true story of Ta-ta, Ta-ta being a kid brother of those two adorable children Ata and Fata, whom we've had occasion to meet and get to know and love. We shall learn, among other things, of why Ta-ta was called Ta-ta.

Ata and Fata went to the best school in the city—the NCP School—which stood, in English, for the National Cultural Premier School and, in Tamil, for the Nallathur Chakrapani and Parvathiammal School (after its founder's parents). Even as you enter the great front portal of the NCP School, you will encounter a huge and lifelike image, from the facing wall, of Sir Nallathur Chakrapani Iyer (in a turban) scowling hideously at you: if you can survive that, you can deal with virtually anything else in later life. This is why the students that passed out of NCP School were among the toughest eggs that ever entered the Indian Administrative Service, or ended up cutting other people's throats, the two being pretty much one and the same thing. But let's get on with the story, for I can see that you are itching to learn of what happened to Ta-ta, and that your inquisitive little minds are bursting with notions of how, and why, and where, and all those eternally endearing questions which make your Mummy and Daddy want to strangle you (and they would, too, take it from me, if they were sure no one was looking).

Well, then. Since Ata and Fata went to the best school in town, it was only natural that Ta-ta's Mummy and Daddy should be as terribly anxious as they were that Ta-ta, too, should go to the same school. Only, getting admission into NCP School was as tough as tough could be. It had been hard enough for Fata and Ata, but as the years went by and Ta-ta appeared on the scene, things had got infinitely harder. Indeed, Ta-ta was registered at NCP School just as soon as his conception was confirmed (and his sex determined). But registration at conception was only a necessary, not sufficient, condition for admission. The candidate, at age three, had to pass a written test on the subject of 'Our Country'. To have a halfway decent chance of passing the test, the child had to be made over, at birth, to the charge of the National Cultural Premier Tutorial Coaching Centre for a period of three years (the Founder of the NCP School, you see, had discovered all about interlocking factor markets long before that economist uncle, Amit Bhaduri, wrote on the subject in the *Cambridge Journal of Economics*). Upfront, you had to pay fifteen lakh rupees for the coaching classes, fifteen lakh for sitting the entrance test, and—if you should pass the test—a further fifteen lakh for admission, by way of a decapitation fee (no cheques accepted).

As soon as the child was born, the NCP Tutorial Coaching Centre's Principal was at the hospital gate, and Mummy and Daddy and Fata and Ata had to bid the child a tearful farewell—which is why he came to be called Ta-ta. At the Coaching Centre, Ta-ta had a whale of a time for three years. Things were, of course, a little different from what you might have expected from a reading of 'Plumfield' in Louisa Alcott's *Little Men*. But at the Centre, they had their own national and cultural schemes for merriment and jollification. The wards were put on a starvation diet for the refinement of their minds, they were treated to the joys of continuous ritual chanting for the refinement of their spirit, they were ducked several times a day in the cold water of the community well to cure them of lust, and, additionally, there was a fair amount of hectic corporal punishment to make it all not just bearable but worthwhile and indeed genuinely amusing for the tutors. But most of all, the infants had to be taught and coached and drilled for the School Entrance Test. The tutors were thorough in their instruction, for which they employed a set of books written by experts who had been specially commissioned for the purpose by the NCERT (National Council for Extreme Rote-learning through Textual-traumatization). Indeed, the NCERT had a comprehensive coaching kit for each pupil, complete with textbooks, thumbscrews and dental drills. Ta-ta's Mummy and Daddy couldn't possibly have been expected to do better by Ta-ta.

Eventually, Ta-ta's third birthday arrived. It was also the day of the Entrance Test. Here's a reproduction of the question paper on the subject of 'Our Country' and the answers our little scholar wrote on that fateful day:

Q1. Who discovered our country?

A1. Vasco da Rama.

Q2. Where was He born?

A2. At the *Janmasthan.*

Q3. Why?

A3. So as to justify the subsequent demolition of the other community's place of worship built on it.

Q4. Who is a member of the other community?

A4. A person who does not observe national mourning when a Pakistani batsman scores a boundary.

Q5. What is the sex ratio of the other community?

A5. 4000 females for every 1000 males.

Q6. Why?

A6. Because every man in the other community marries four women.

Q7.  Which is the only minority community in our country?

A7.  Mine. It accounts for four per cent of the population, but only fifty per cent of all the Prime Ministers we have had, thirty-five per cent of all Secretarial positions in Government, and forty per cent of all executive posts in Public Sector Corporations.

Q8.  Why is our Prime Minister so sweet?

A8.  Becauthe he lithpth.

Q9.  Write a patriotic essay, derived from media-appreciation, on 'My Country' in two sentences.

A9.  My Country—A Patriotic Essay in Two Sentences
Sentence 1: I love my India.
Sentence 2: Come on, India.

Q10. What is our National Colour?

A10. Saphron.

Alas! Alas! It was a near-perfect ten, but Ta-ta, as you can see, slipped up fearfully on the last question, by being oversubtle when it came to spelling 'saffron'. For this brilliant little boy, nine on ten wasn't enough to make the grade: thanks to horrid men like the B.P. Mandal and V.P. Singh I've mentioned earlier, there was an iniquitous thing called Reservation whereby a child like Ta-ta belonging to the 'Forward Community' had to score ten on ten in order to qualify, whereas 'Backwards' only had to score nine on ten, which explains why there's no respect for merit in our country and there's so much inefficiency and we have to be so ashamed when President Clinton visits us.

Ta-ta's Mummy and Daddy and their entire community deplored the caste system in our country bitterly, and wrote many passionate letters to that effect to the Editor of *The Hindu*. Naturally, Mummy and Daddy couldn't bear the shame of their child's failure, and they threw him out of the house, to be brought up in a reform school. In course of time Ta-ta learnt to accept his inferior position in the scheme of things, though, having got it wrong the first time

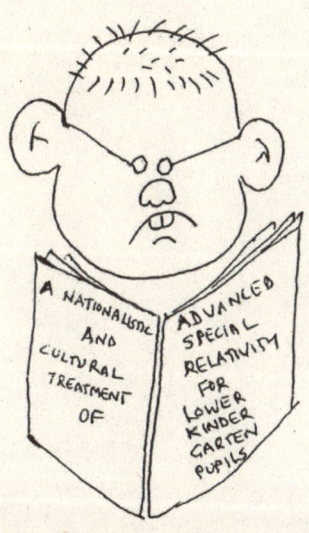

he continued to get it wrong, by overcompensating: he always maintained that Mummy's and Daddy's discriminatory attitude had left him feeling 'offraned', by which he meant 'orphaned'.

Children, I hope you've learnt what a terrible thing caste discrimination is. Though, if things should get too bad here, there's always the prospect of Silicon Valley, where they don't have silly things like Reservation. But in any event, dimwits, there's no harm in using spellcheck.

# 5
## Field Studies and Inter-Disciplinarity

Whimsy in the Woods
(or)
Arcadia in the Academy

Winnie-the-Goo was called Winnie-the-Goo because he was a winsome bear of glutinous charm. His best friend was Sunflower Sobbin. Sunflower Sobbin could be relied upon to bring a happy-sad lump to your throat every time (which was all the time) he addressed Goo Bear in the endearing terms of 'Silly old Bear'. *Most* of the time, Winnie-the-Goo was a bear of little brain, and when he wasn't that, he was a bear of no brain at all. But all that changed after his visit to India. *Then*, he became a bear of considerable brain. So Considerable indeed, as it turned out, that upon his return to the Enchanted Place, he was promptly offered an Endowered Chair. This wasn't just any old chair; it was the Chair of Cultural Ethnopology at the University of Somesex. The Chair was a very special chair, because it was a gift from the Overlapping Disciplinary Institution for Outstandingly Underhanded Scholarship (O.D.I.O.U.S for short).

From the Hundred Acre Wood to the Mudumalai Forest is a very long way, and it's a journey that is not ordinarily within the Realm of Practical Politics. How it came to pass was like this. At the end of a certain financial year (just as at the end of every other financial year), the ex-Imperial Council in the city of Chennai found itself with a lot of undisbursed funds on its hands. This happened because the staff of the Council had been so very busy, over the rest of the year, chasing up other things, if 'Things', indeed, is a politically correct word for Popsies. Given the Exigencies Of The Circumstances it was confronted by, the Council promptly decided to organize a very expensive Cultural Exchange Programme. Whether or not there was much Cultural Exchange involved, there certainly was a satisfyingly good deal of Foreign Exchange mixed up in it. And so it happened that Goo Bear and his friends Sunflower Sobbin, Snigger, Pigling, Grabit, and Eyesore found themselves, at a certain date, in the Mudumalai Forest, making the acquaintance of Karadi the Bear, Puli the Tiger, Panni the Pig, Muyal the Rabbit, Kazhuthai the Ass, Nari the Fox, Korangu the Monkey, Mynah the mynah, and all the other creatures of the Forest.

Goo Bear and his friends did themselves well in the matter of nutrition on their first evening in the Forest, even though Goo, being a polite and courteous bear, was anxious not to appear greedy. Still, he couldn't *quite* control himself when the alcoholic stimulant was passed around. He discovered that he had an Unquenchable Thirst for what the natives called *arrack*, mixed with substantial dollops of honey. Ordinarily a bear that couldn't say Boo to a Goose, he became a wholly different animal when it came to a question of separating Goo from the Booze: wild elephants couldn't keep him from it. While gentle snores broke the still quietness around the forest campfire, Goo Bear, still under the influence, came to life: his little brain became very large, and he sat up, even as he entered into a Thoughtful Frame of mind.

'I have', he announced, 'been thinking. In fact, I've just had an In-, In-, Insurrection.'

'Silly old Bear', said Sunflower Sobbin tenderly, rubbing the sleep from his eyes. '"Inspiration" is what you mean.'

'Well, that, then', said Goo. 'Or what you might call a brainwave, if you chose to.'

'Or not, as the case may be', said Eyesore, in his negative and dispirited way, despite, Paradoxically, having a muchness of the spirits in his system.

'Will the wave engulf us?' asked Pigling, shrinking.

'It would help to hear about it', said Snigger.

'Well', said Goo in his Gravest Voice, 'It is my careful and considered decision', said Goo Most Solemnly, 'that I should become an Epidemic', said Goo with Utmost Earnestness. 'Er ... books, you know', he added, 'and reading, and writing, and such things, you know.'

'Silly old Bear', said Sunflower Sobbin fondly, '"Academic" is what you're after.'

'Yes', said Goo, thanking Sunflower Sobbin in his courteous way, before suddenly breaking into song:

*I'll put the wretched b-gg-s to work,*
*While myself sitting back to smirk:*
*Umty-tumty, tumty-tum,*
*Tra-la, la-la, la-la, la-la.*
*Let 'em gather the bricks and mortar,*
*Run around and fetch the data,*
*While the credit for the magnum opus*
*Comes to us, to us, to us, to us.*
*To us, (or me), the royalty,*
*The name, the fame, in perpetuity:*
*Let the coolies toil and spin*
*So that I may rake the profits in.*
*Tra-la, la-la, la-la, la-la,*
*Umty-tumty, tiddly-pum.*

And Goo was as good as his word. The very next morning, he realized that the first thing he needed to do was to establish a contact. Nari the Fox was the ideal candidate. Only, Nari first insisted, through various forms of indirection, that he needed to be Propitiated before he could be expected to Oblige. This was not a very difficult thing to do. Sunflower Sobbin had an uncle who was something of a grandee at the University of Somesex, and it was a simple enough matter to arrange with him to arrange for Nari to spend six weeks at Somesex on a training programme for Disaster Management in the Third World. Nari was given a miniscule subsistence allowance with which he was quite content, because the pound is very strong and the rupee is very weak. What's more, the training programme made no demands on Nari, which was most convenient for him, since it left him with all the time in the world to indulge his favourite passion, which was to do a thorough survey of all the sex shops around the University.

To cut a long story short, Nari the Fox proved to be a source of invaluable help to Winnie-the-Goo. He recruited Tavalai the Toad (Beneath-the-Harrow) to organize an entire army of field workers, consisting of several of Korangu the Monkey's friends and relatives, who were happy to work in exchange for a pittance and a kind word from 'Goo Sar', as they called Winnie-the-Goo. Soon they busied themselves with questionnaires and interview schedules and headcounts and surveys, which Goo was glad to leave to them to handle, since these things added up, as he knew very well, to rather inferior skills which he, as a bear of considerable brain, was naturally above. (Every now and then, it's regrettable to say, the field workers got up to monkey tricks: on particularly hot or rainy days, they just hung about, scratching their back and front sides, and cooking up numbers, as their fancy seized them, which went into the schedules. Goo had a vague suspicion of these Goings-on, but he didn't care an awful lot, because he knew that nobody back home would be any the wiser.) The superior skills that were needed, Goo told himself, were those that would go into the Processing, Analysis and Theorizing of the data. This would have to wait till the field work was completed, and until it was, Goo busied himself cracking the whip at Nari and Tavalai, amidst desultory bouts of stoutness exercises and active bouts of country beer.

Suddenly one day, without so much as a warning, the field work came to an end. It was now up to Goo to do the Processing, Analysis and Theorizing.

'Oh, help!' said Goo.
'Oh, bother!' said Goo.
'Oh, help *and* bother!' said Goo.

Just then, Goo's eyes lighted upon the sleepy figure of Andhai the Owl. Andhai the Owl was a very clever, very lazy, and very vain owl. Goo plied the old oil assiduously. By dint of cunning stratagem and unremitting flattery, he succeeded, while pretending to pick berries, in picking Andhai the Owl's brain. Andhai, over numerous sessions, did all the Processing and Analysis and Theorizing, while Goo made sure that Korangu and the rest took notes in longhand.

Then it was that Goo's books started emerging, not to say rolling out, one after the other. The University Presses at Poxford and Scam-bridge, Weasel Whitewell, Hank Crass, Rottage, they all tripped, and scrabbled, and elbowed each other out of the way to get at Goo's books and publish them. With all this attention, Goo became, as it were, and so to speak, bolder by the book. The first one was called *Gender Imbalance and Kinky Kinships in Mudumalai*; the second, *Patrons, Clients, and the Immoral Economy in South India*; the third, *Meals, Moods, and Morbidity in India*; and the fourth, *Irrigation, Mortality, Infrastructure, Politics, Ecology, Civil Society, Fertility, and Everything Else in Asia*. There was no stopping Goo now. He realized that 'Cultural Ethnopology' is what Cultural Ethnopologists do, and he could think of no good reason why a Cultural Ethnopologist shouldn't do just what it pleased him (that is to say, him/her) to do. Apart from which, there was still the large, untapped postmodern market waiting to be worked. This was the inspiration for Goo's most famous book, which was based on an entirely fake interview with the dreaded forest bandit, Meesai the Moustache. He called it *Culture, Development, and Popular Cinema: Pederasty, Subalternity, and Brigandry in the Third World*.

Winnie-the-Goo and his friends have only just begun. There is still so much left to be done. I give you my word that we shall accompany them on their expotitions in Burkina Faso, in Papua New Guinea, in Cote d'Ivoire, in Bangladesh, ... Meanwhile, it is my earnest hope that every little friend that has read this little tale will have been enabled to give a wholly unambiguous answer to old Mr Bertrand Russell's favourite question in moral philosophy: Which would you rather be: a bear of little brain, or a bear of no scruple?

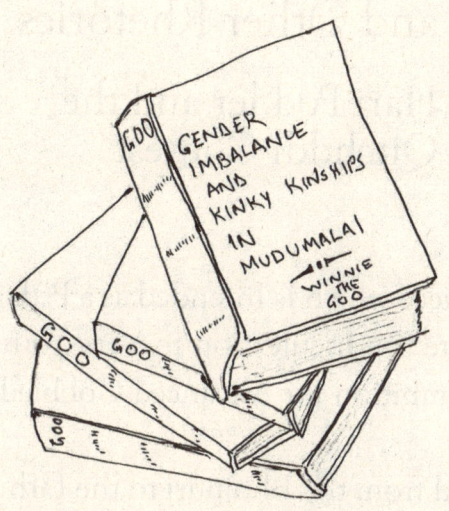

# 6

## The Rhetoric of Economics and Other Rhetorics

### Hari Podder and the Qitchddi Contest

[Being a Piece which is Intended as a Pedagogical Aid to Facilitate the Inculcation in Very Young Scholars of Early Ambition for Advanced Gobbledygookery]

\*\*\*

[Translated from the Bhojpuri to the Lithuanian and thence to English]

H ari Podder was an eleven-year-old who, thanks to the evil machinations of the Unmentionable One (him of the Dark Side), had in early infancy lost his parents and gained a scar. Running, as it did, a few times round his face, the scar marked him out as the chosen one, for the great role he was destined to play in the events to come. For, when you came right down to it, Hari wasn't one of the Makkals he lived amongst, he was a wizard.

Makkals, as you know (or should, if you have any Tamil), are the *hoi polloi*; and they didn't come any beastlier (until you counted their son) than the aunt and uncle on whom Hari was dumped by his parents' wizard friends. For nearly eleven years, Hari was brought up by his awful relatives in a toilet (Indian style). This resulted in some water in the brain, which explains why he had no notion of his own magical powers. Otherwise, he should certainly have suspected he wasn't quite a normal child, considering he had been able to survive his aunt's cooking all those years.

It was only on his eleventh birthday that Hari learnt of his wizard origins, from an unwashed and dimwitted giant who suddenly descended, astride a Hero Honda, from a cloud of owls. This somewhat weird personage then equipped the boy with a wand and a broom (a wonderful new Sweeper

Six Thousand), and carried him off to Swot Ghar, pausing, on the way, only to pick up for himself a half dozen bottles of Haywards Five Thousand.

The Chancellor of the International Group of Swotschools was one of the greatest wizards of all time. (It should be mentioned that every major city in the world had a Swotschool. In London, it was called Swot House; in Paris, Swot Maison; in San Francisco, Swot Pad; and along the same general lines elsewhere.) The Chancellor's sleepy, senile, absent-minded face and immense, spherical, baggy posterior frequently appeared on (and disappeared from) the wrappers of Wizard Candy Treat Bars, which, in the post-globalization era, became easily available to wizards in an invisible side street extension of Chor Bazaar. From these wrappers Hari learnt that, among other things, the great Allbutt Fumblesnore was the celebrated author of *Hermeneutics of Magic Realism* and *The Great Vanishing Trick: Deconstructing the Absent Other*.

On Hari's first day at Swot Ghar, Fumblesnore personally presided over the assignment of all the new pupils to their respective School Houses. There were three Houses: Stormpendo, Starmix, and Elclassicano.* Hari was assigned to Stormpendo

---

* Those well-versed in Hari Podder literature cannot have failed to run into Allbutt Fumblesnore's classic work on

along with his friend Hiranmoyee. Jhanda Lal, one of the two rudest and most offensive boys in school, was assigned to Starmix, while his nearest rival to this distinction, the slimy Anartha Sankhya Shastri, drew Elclassicano.

The head of Stormpendo was a prodigiously clever scholar who taught a course in *Secret Writing through Destructive Reading*. She was a highly non-trivial person, and could be particularly severe on you if you expressed yourself badly such as, for instance, by suggesting that you sometimes found it difficult to tell your left hand from your right, when what you really meant was that the negotiation of binary oppositions was a fraught event. Starmix was headed by a Professor who taught *Elements of Transformation* and, to prove the point, sported a beard of awesome luxuriance, which was rather a shame, since all that extensive foliage concealed a first-class and permanent sneer. He was very good at haranguing people and telling them, loudly and incessantly, what they should or shouldn't be doing. Head of Elclassicano was a sinister and wild-eyed Professor, who strove

---

*Anagrams, Spells and Potions*, from which it can be easily verified that 'Swot Ghar' is a jumbled version of 'wart hogs' (as also, of course, of Hogwarts), just as 'Stormpendo', 'Starmix' and 'Elclassicano' are jumbled versions of, respectively, 'Postmodern', 'Marxist', and 'Neoclassical'.

hard to put everything into axioms and equations and formulas. When anything refused to let itself be reduced to one of his neat little squiggles, he lost his temper, and, with a vicious wave of his wand, wished it away, on the ground that the wretched thing was exogenous to his model. He taught *Economicstricks for Beginners*.

From day to day there were many other things, apart from the mandatory swotting, which kept Hari and his friends busy, such as exploring forbidden rooms, being chased by slavering three-headed dogs, avoiding deadly traps laid for them by the Unmentionable One's agents, and similar compulsory adventures which you can yourselves supply from your close, website acquaintance with this genre of children's fiction. The one thing, however, which kept them the busiest, was the alarming rate at which the Starmix and the Elclassicano tutors kept deducting points from the Stormpendo tally, on one pretext or another.

On one occasion, when the Starmix tutor saw Hari muttering to himself (he was trying to memorize a spell for an exam), he accused the boy of praying, and promptly deducted fifty points from Stormpendo. He deducted points from various other Stormpendians for being Obscurantist, Bourgeois, Petty-Bourgeois, Peasant, and Imperialist, and he deducted twice as many points for their failure to be Modern, Radical, Scientific, Progressive, and Internationalist. When he ran out of points to withdraw, he docked the Stormpendians' pocket money in the larger cause which sanctioned an egalitarian redistribution of resources (that is to say, to himself). He virtually wiped Stormpendo clean when he suddenly picked on Hiranmoyee and asked her to name a popular Stormpendo folk hero who had written on lunatic asylums and power. This was easy pickings for Hiranmoyee, the most prominent swotter in her class, but when she said 'Foucault!', the Starmix tutor immediately erased three hundred points from the Stormpendo score on the grounds that Hiranmoyee had uttered an expletive in just after the fashion that Geoffrey Boycott might have done.

The Elclassicano tutor didn't prove to be any easier to deal with. He penalized Hari for allegedly possessing a budget set that was not a convex polyhedron, Hiranmoyee for displaying behaviour incompatible with the Weak Axiom of Revealed Preference, and a third Stormpendian for eating his House badge. Worst of all was when he caught a young Stormpendo scholar sneaking cigarettes from Gasper the Friendly Ghost. What with one thing and another, it became clear that if Stormpendo was to have the remotest chance of coming out on top that year, they would just have to win the annual Qitchddi* contest.

Qitchddi was a word salad game that is a staple of every Hari Podder story. The captain of each team was shrouded in a magic mantle which made him invisible to all but the captains of the other teams. Each captain was assisted by any number of Prompters from his team, who fed him with hexes, spells, incantations, jargon, and other forms of mumbo jumbo which he would call out, in rotation, the idea being to try and unseat, through the sheer power of his mumbo jumbo, the captains of the other teams from their respective broomsticks. As an additional aid, each captain was also allowed to clout, wallop, prod, etc. the other captains with his broomstick. The mumbo jumbo was calculated, in stages, to Transfigure the opponent to his true form, and if your true form wasn't conducive to straddling a broomstick, well, that was too bad for you.

Hari Podder was the captain of Stormpendo. Starmix and Elclassicano cheated straightaway:

---

* 'Khichri? Yuck. That's the standard response to the most maligned dish in the subcontinent... It's a synonym for an inelegant mish-mash, an unappetizing jumble.' This is Jug Suraiya on Khichri (or Qitchddi as I spell it): see his 'How to Make a Khichri' in his column *Jugular Vein* in the *Times of India* of 1 March 2003.

Jhanda Lal and Anartha Sankhya Shastri, the captains, respectively, of these two Houses, tipped their broomsticks with nasty, pointed ends, and took refuge in their invisibility-producing mantles to cover their dirty trick. Allbutt Fumblesnore, who never missed an annual Qitchddi contest in whichever part of the world it may be hosted, presided over the toss. The order of precedence turned out to be: first, Starmix; second, Elclassicano; and third, Stormpendo. It was in this order that the mumbo jumbo was called out, to the accompaniment of many clearly foul prods in Hari's ribs by Jhanda Lal and Sankhya Shastri. However, Hari just about managed to hold on to his broomstick, while Hiranmoyee and her friends fed him with mumbo after jumbo. The first three rounds went like this (in the order of Starmix, Elclassicano, and Stormpendo):

'Surpluslabour!
'Rybzhinski Theorem!'
'Aporia!'

'Historicaldialecticalmaterialism!'
'Strictly quasi-concave function!'
'Gendered subjectivity!'

'Formalsubsumptionoflabourundercapital!'
'Kalai-Smorodinsky equilibria in epsilon environments with compact, non-convex sets!'

'*Jouissance, différence, materialité, localité,* hegemony, patriarchy, metanarrative, cyborg, resistance, agency, embodied subjects, the subject as body, the body as subject, space, spaces, private spaces, public spaces!'

At this point, an accident occurred, which reduced the field of contestants to Stormpendo and Elclassicano: for, quite suddenly, the Soviet Union collapsed all over, about, and upon Jhanda Lal, thereby rendering him *hors de combat.* The Qitchddi tournament continued through several more exhausting rounds, which it would take too many pages to describe. Suffice to say that as the game wore on, both Sankhya Shastri and Hari Podder were gradually transfigured, to the horror of both, into the increasingly recognizable forms of a pair of warthogs, making it virtually impossible for them to hold on to their respective broomsticks. When all that was left for the final transfiguration to occur was a wriggly tail apiece, each team delved deep into its repository of incantations to come up with one last, desperate, powerful item of mumbo jumbo. Sankhya Shastri came up with the following hex from the Elclassicano Grand Wizard, Paul Samuelson, who had authored it when he was in an autobiographical mood:

Again, *Foundations* innovated the then-new concept of *quasi*-definiteness for an n-squared matrix [aij] ... My

German text gives page references that dispel mystery about a failure in *Foundations* to employ the rudimentary Lyapunov technique. My actual 1947 explicit references to Alexander Lyapunov, Emile Picard, and Birkhoff had mostly to do with the more delicate cases of borderline stability related to measure-preserving conservative Hamiltonian and more general systems; prior to the 1960s breakthrough in chaos theory, I, in the late 1930s was too unsophisticated to grapple with Henri Poincare, George Birkhoff, Edward Lorenz, and Stephen Smale subtleties.*

Hari's tail was just beginning to sprout under this onslaught, when Hiranmoyee managed to save the day with the following indescribable item of Metaqitchddi from the work of the Most High and Exalted Grand Wizard of Stormpendo, Jacques Derrida:

But why is *all this* explained precisely *in prefaces?* What is the status of this third term which cannot *simply*, as a *text*, be either inside philosophy or outside it, neither in the markings, nor in the matchings, nor in the margins of the book? This term that is never sublated by the dialectical method without having a remainder? That is neither a pure form, completely empty, given it *announces* the path and semantic production of the concept, nor a content, a moment of meaning, since it remains external to the

---

* Paul A. Samuelson, 1998, 'How Foundations Came to Be', *Journal of Economic Literature*, 36(3): 1375–86.

logos of which it indefinitely feeds the critique, if only through the gap between ratiocination and rationality, between empirical history and conceptual history? If one sets out from the oppositions—form/content, signifier/signified, sensible/intelligible—one cannot comprehend the writing of a preface. But in thus *remaining*, does a preface *exist*? Its spacing (the preface to a rereading) diverges in (the) place of the χώρα.*

This was too much for Sankhya Shastri. A perfect hog's tail emerged from the base of his spine, as with one last despairing squeal, he fell from his broomstick to the ground. Learning and impenetrability had triumphed! The contest had been decided, if not by a whisker, then by one short hog's tail! Stormpendo had won the annual Qitchddi contest, and with that, the House Medal!

* Jacques Derrida, 1981, *Dissemination*, translated by Barbara Johnson, Chicago: University of Chicago Press, pp. 15–16.

# 7
## Pedagogy in Economics
## 1936 and All That*

*[In view of British economists' inability to predict the global crisis (vide HM the Queen's concerns in the matter), it is*

* An edited and abbreviated version of this piece appeared in the *Royal Economic Society Newsletter*, Issue 148: 17, January–March 2010.

*clear that the teaching of economics in the country is in urgent*
*need of improvement. The subject of economics education*
*was also taken up for elaborate discussion in the previous*
*(October/December 2009) issue of this newsletter. The*
*present contribution carries that project forward, drawing*
*inspiration from the work of two eminent educationists of*
*an earlier era, W. C. Sellar and R. J. Yeatman. Indeed,*
*the RES may wish to invite other economists to submit*
*their own test papers, toward the laudable pedagogic end of*
*building a substantial and distinguished question bank for*
*the benefit of future generations of economics scholars.]*

— • —

## *Test Paper 1: Revision Questions*

Answer every other question, beginning with
Question 2 and ignoring all even-numbered items.
As students training to be economists, you are
encouraged—indeed, expected—to display a wide
range of sharp practice.

1. Which is better, a Marshallian Cross or a Pigouvian
Tax? Why not? If not, why? (In either case, use only a
Geometric Argument.)

2. Explain, in not less than 20,000 words, the
irretrievable Theoretical Consequences of combining
Quasi-transitive Rationality with a Cobb-Douglas
Production Function. Would it be worth the risk?
(Crib like hell.)

3. (a) What, employing parliamentary language only, would you do with a Sub-Game Perfect Equilibrium? (b) To whom? [You may answer either (a) or (b), or neither, but not both.]

4. Can you compare and contrast the Slutsky Effect and the Rybczynski Theorem? Well then, what *can* you do with them? (Answer only in Ukrainian or Polish.)

5. (This question is for Economic Historians.) Seriously now, how far would you go to stab a mathematical economist? (Be sure to use a divider.)

6. Why do you know anything of Granger Causality? (Or of Giardia Entiritis, for that matter?)

7. Which turns you on more: a Discriminating Monopolist or a Kinked Demand Curve? (Try not to be explicit.)

8. Which would you try and get away with, if you could: an $R^2$ of (–)1 or an $R^2$ of 2.0? (Be utterly devious.)

9. If you saw a picture of Karl Marx and one of a Social Welfare Function, how long would it take you to tell the one from the other? (Quickly, now.)

10. If that was easy, try this one. If you saw a picture of Karl Marx and one of Grigori Rasputin, how long

would it take you to tell the one from the other?
(Frankly, now.)

11. Money is super-neutral to a Monetarist, but can a
Monetarist ever be super-neutral to Money? Or even
ordinarily neutral? (What is it about money? Explain
in loving detail.)

12. Which of these two episodes of *Doctor Who* did
you like best: 'Random Walk' or 'White Noise?'
(Think carefully before answering. At any rate, answer
carefully before thinking.)

13. Arrange, in descending order of unpleasantness:
(a) An Inflationary Spiral; (b) A Knife-edge
Equilibrium; (c) The Natural Rate of Unemployment;
(d) A Liquidity Trap; (e) The Great Depression; and
(f) The Ashes Series. Give reasons for your ranking,
writing on not more than two sides of the paper, and
stating clearly if you are English or Australian, when
not either. (Be unreasonable.)

14. Castigate impartially each of the following pairs
of Menaces to Civil Society: (a) Stolper-Samuelson;
(b) Durbin-Watson; (c) Harrod-Domar; (d) Heckscher-
Ohlin; (e) Kalai-Smorodinsky; and (f) The Bobbsey
Twins. (Be intemperate.)

15. Why is being an economist a Bad Thing for
Everyone Else?

OR

Annotate, with reference to the context, Nigel Molesworth's observation: 'Ekonomysts are calkellaters and sofisters (posh prose, hem-hem), e.g. snekes, cads and roters chiz chiz chiz.'

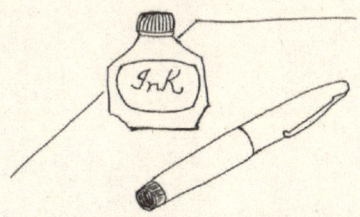

## Old Favourites

All these books are the majestic expressions
of the universal conscience, and are more to
our daily purpose than this year's almanac
or this day's newspaper.

—R.W. Emerson
('Books', in *Society and Solitude*,
p. 208, Houghton, Miffin and
Company, Boston, 1887)

# 8
## Games and
## Economic Behaviour
### Brer Rabbit and
### the Cricket Match*

W hen tellyvishun done gone come to de briar
patch, ole Brer Rabbit, he become mighty

* This piece originally appeared, under the same title, in *The Hindu*'s Sunday Magazine of 11 February 2001.

watchful. He watch de tellyvishun from mornin' till night, an' he larnt himself a whole lot of new t'ings which de rest of de critters was too dumb to larn. Of all de t'ings Brer Rabbit saw, what took his fancy mos' was dis new game he ain't never knowed nothin' 'bout befo', callt cricket. He lay low an' he watch an' bimeby he become mighty thoughtful. Wit' a mind as crafty as a cartload of monkeys, he reckoned that nobody could teach him no new tricks, but he changed his mind quick about dat when he see dis t'ing callt match-fixin'. 'Here', he sez to himself, 'is somet'in' new an' full of promise.' An' he sets himself to work.

Soon Brer Rabbit, he spreads cricket all over de place. All de little critters is crazy 'bout de game, an' not long after, so's all de chilluns' Mammies an' Pappies. Befo' you knows it, dere's two Internash'nal Teams, de Bears an' de Foxes, an' dey's at each udder's t'roats, which suits Brer Rabbit fine, 'cos now he kin have some peace an' quiet, wit' Brer Bear (de captin of de Bears) an' Brer Fox (de captin of de Foxes) at loggerhaids wit' each udder. Brer Rabbit, he appoint himself as coach an' manager' an' sponsor an' Praz'dent an' Wise-Praz'dent of de Cricket Council an' umpire an' bookie all rollt into one, an' he have himself a mighty fine time. Ev'y now an' den Brer Rabbit ain't none too sho' 'bout de rules of de game, but he never lets on, an' he never 'low dat to come in de way of nothin', 'cos he's quick to make his own rules as he go along. Bimeby de day draws near fer de Fust Cricket Test Match between de Bears an' de Foxes.

De day befo' de match, Brer Rabbit keep himself busy fillin' up ten jars wit' glue an' addin' a spot of yaller colorin' to it. He den sticks a label wit' 'HUNNY' printed on it on each jar, an' he makes sho' Brer Bear gets to see de jars as he walks him past his house. Brer Bear's eyes, dey full of greed for de 'hunny', an' his stummick, it rumbles at de sight. Dat night, Brer Bear is in a agony of longin' for de honey, when he sudd'nly gets a tellyphone call from Brer Rabbit. Brer Rabbit, he wants to make a deal wit' Brer Bear. Brer Bear has to call at de toss nex' mawnin', an' Brer Rabbit, who has a one-sided coin will make sho' dat Brer Bear wins de toss. Brer Bear has to bat fust an' t'row de match away makin' sho' dat de Bears makes jest a hunnerd runs. Dat's in exchange for de ten jars of honey. Brer Bear, he ax his conshunce an' he ax his stummick, an' since he ain't got de one an' he do have de udder, he agrees to de deal. Before all dis happen, Brer Rabbit (who's goin' to umpire de match from bot' ends) has already got a big fat lot of boodle from Brer Fox in exchange for makin' sho' dat Brer Rabbit won't decleer Brer Fox out nex' day. Meanwhile, in de days leadin' up to de match, Brer Rabbit bin mighty busy placin' bets on de outcome. He's got all de critters gamblin' wildly.

Half de critters bet on de Bears winnin', an' de udder half bet on de Foxes winnin'. Brer Rabbit, he bin off'rin' huge odds on bot' sides.

De day of de great match arrive, an' ev'yt'ing go 'cordin' to plan. Brer Bear win de toss and de Bears, dey's skittled out for jest a hunnerd runs. De Foxes bat nex', an' dey reach a hunnerd fer nine wickets, after Brer Fox bin bowled nineteen times an' bin decleered not out nineteen times by Brer Rabbit on account dey was all no-balls. Number Eleven walks in, his knees knockin' togedder, an' lookin' as skeered as a bunny. De scores is level now, an' de Foxes has one run to make to win, an' one wicket in hand, an' all de rest of de afternoon to play. De bowler bowls an' de ball is ten feet wide an' de batter ain't anywheres near it, when Brer Rabbit holler 'Howzzat?' to hisself an' also raises his finger. Out L.B.W.! You should hev sin Brer Fox's face! De match, it done gone ended in a tie! Nobody who bet on de match get to win, an' Brer Rabbit he make a real nice, tidy packet.

Dat evenin', after Brer Bear transfer all de 'hunny' jars from Brer Rabbit's house to his own, de polis blow de whistle on him. Fer dey bin tappin' his tellyphone, an' dey kotched him in de ack. Dey cun't fix nothin' on Brer Rabbit 'cos dat clever animal, he done gone changed his voice when he spoke over de tellyphone wit' Brer Bear. De case landed in court an' Brer Bear tells de judge, pointin' a big, fat, shakin' finger at Brer Rabbit, 'bout how he tried to bribe him wit' all dose jars of honey. De judge has to examine de evidence, an' he scoop out a fingerfull of 'hunny' from de jar an' lick his finger. He don't get no honey in his mouth, only a lot of yaller-colored glue which stick his jaws tight togedder, an' dey won't come apart fer de nex' ten days. De judge is powerful mad, an' jes' as soon as he kin speak, he reads de sentence and t'rows Brer Bear in de slammer. As fer Brer Rabbit, dat cunnin' critter skedaddles off to de bank wit' all de loot he's made, lippity-clippity, clippity-lippity, sayin' to himself, jes' as sassy as a jay-bird, 'Honnisty is de *wuss* pollisy.'

Dere's some 'conomist critters, like ole Brer Groves an' ole Brer Ledyard an' ole Brer Laffont, what's tryin' to figger out when honnisty is de *bess* pollisy. Dey got some mighty fancy names fer it, sump'n dat sound

like 'implementashun' an' "centive contemptibility' an' 'revelashun of pref'rences' or somesech. Dey's still figgerin' it out, an' scratchin' dey haids, an' waitin' fer de Nobul Prize.

Well, honeychile. Dat's it fer tonight. Nex' time roun', I'll tell de story 'bout how to work de Nobul scam.

# 9
## Human Development

### Alice and the Seven Per Cent Solution*

'You think you know everything, don't you?' said
the Mad Hatter, with a sneer.

---

* This piece originally appeared, under the same title, in *The Hindu*'s Sunday Magazine of 15 April 2001.

'I didn't ever say that', protested Alice indignantly.

'I didn't say you did', retorted the Mad Hatter. 'For a girl who believes she knows everything', he continued, 'it should be very easy for you to answer the following question. Given that a straight line is the shortest distance between any two points, and that a Mock Turtle's favourite food is seaweed soup laced with arsenic, what is the largest integer less than twenty-eight which is smaller than the square root of two?'

'I don't believe I've ever heard such nonsense in my life', declared Alice crossly.

'A likely enough excuse for shameful ignorance', said the Mad Hatter, very decidedly.

'It comes from her not knowing her fractions', said the March Hare, shaking his head sadly.

'I do, too, know my fractions', muttered the Dormouse, opening one eye. 'A quarter and a quarter make an eighth', he added, before falling asleep again.

'Two cups of tea for the Dormouse!' cried the Mad Hatter. 'One for getting the sum right, and one for getting the person that doesn't know her fractions wrong.'

'We'll have to send her to the Indian Middleman to help her get her fractions right', said the March Hare, while carrying out the Mad Hatter's instruction, by pouring first one cup of tea, and then another, over the Dormouse.

'The Indian Middleman!' cried the Mad Hatter, the March Hare, and the Dormouse, all together. And before she knew what they were about, they had pushed a bewildered Alice down a hole in the ground.

After what seemed like an interminable journey through an interminable tunnel, Alice eventually emerged into a room which had a single occupant in it. The occupant was a very fat pig, which on closer inspection revealed itself to be a remarkably pig-like human, dressed in a suit, and seated in front of a table. On the table were several plates of salted nuts and various other spicy foods, and also a large bottle with an amber fluid in it, and a half-filled glass next to it. The pig-man drank out of the glass and ate out of all the plates, first clockwise, and then counterclockwise. Alice was fascinated by the speed, the efficiency, and the noises with which the food and the drink were vanishing. Without interrupting himself in his drinking and eating, the pig-man stared at Alice. If she had known the word, Alice would have described his stare as a lecherous one. She finally broke the awkward silence.

'Are you', she enquired timidly, 'the Indian Middleman?'

The pig-man stuffed his mouth with food, chewed deliberately, and washed it down with a draught from his glass, before bothering to reply.

'Maybe', he said. 'Who you are?'

'My name', replied Alice truthfully, 'is Alice. What's yours, if I may ask?'

'SK – PK – TK – KK – something like that. I've forgotten myself. So many shady deals, one after another, you forget your own name. OK. You can call me Some-K.'

'How do you do, Mr Some-K?'

'How? Simpal. You give. I do.'

'I'm afraid I don't quite understand, Mr Some-K', said Alice, who was beginning to feel very confused. 'What am I supposed to give?'

'Standard', replied the Middleman promptly. 'No negotiations. Seven per cent. But quality has to be little OK, OK? You have to make sure on this. When product is coming for tests, it cannot able to fail more than seven trials out of eight. Clear message from Highest Quarter, routed through HQO.'

'And what' asked Alice, though she didn't understand a single thing of what the Middleman had just said, 'is the message?'

'Nathional defenthe thecurity mutht not be compromithed', said the Middleman.

'Why does the Highest Quarter speak like that?' asked Alice curiously.

'Cute', said the Middleman. 'Pippal like leader who is lisping. Make him papoolar leader.'

There was a brief silence while Alice reflected on the Middleman's remarks. While she was still thinking, he spoke again.

'Drink?' he said.

'We-ell', said Alice doubtfully. 'It depends on what you have.'

'Whisky', replied the Middleman. 'Best. Bloody Blue Label. From Bukhoi deal. Two more bottles at home. One from Pig deal, one from Sarak deal. Help yourself.'

'Thank you', said Alice very civilly, 'but I think I'd much rather not, if you don't mind.' She had no idea what she was being offered, but all the things she had eaten or drunk so far had had such strange results that she decided she wouldn't tempt providence again.

'So, OK', said the Middleman. 'I fix the deal for you. First advance, then I finish the job, balance after that. What your line is? Artillery?'

Alice did not have the faintest notion of what the Middleman meant.

'I'm afraid I don't quite follow you, Mr Some-K', she said helplessly.

'No need pretend', said the Middleman reassuringly. 'I am knowing everything. You are in arms trade, no?'

'I'm in nothing of the sort', said Alice angrily.

'Then in flesh trade?' leered the Middleman.

Before Alice could respond to this outrageous suggestion, the Middleman was off again. 'See here', he said. 'I am knowing everything. You are representative of East End Armament Corporation. You are living in London, Manchester United Street. We can open LC with your London banker, Thomas Cook. You are flying to India by Nat West Airlines. You are having MBA degree from Cambridge School of Economics. So, everything is known, no need for shy. Let us conclude. You are willing for giving seven per cent?'

Alice's head was spinning at an alarming rate. All she was able to say, feebly, was: 'Whatever for, Mr Some-K?'

'Arre, when everybody take, I have to give everybody, no? Principal Party President, three per cent; Coalition Party Secretary, two per cent; this-that bureaucrat, two per cent; Defence pippal, General-Shenerals, one per cent; *chaprassi* to Personal Assistant to Personal Secretary to Special Secretary to Highest Quarter, quarter per cent. And, after all, bloody myself also, no? Another half per cent. Not to forget inflation, quarter per cent. So you add up.'

Alice concentrated very hard on adding up. She did it three times over. Sums always tired her out, and when she knew she had added as much as she possibly could without risking a fever, she told the Middleman very humbly:

'Well, Mr Some-K, I know I'm not very good at fractions and such things, which is why I've been sent here in the first place by the Mad Hatter and the other creatures, but do please tell me why it is that the numbers you have mentioned add up to nine per cent, and not seven per cent.'

'Arre, what to do?' said the Middleman, cramming nineteen thoughtful peanuts into his mouth. 'This is India. When so many pippal take, we have to give to all. So the numbers are adding up more and more. Hundred crore pippal in the country. How the numbers won't add up? So Revamped Self-Serving Sect—RSS—they are giving sanction for new formula from Vedic Mathematics: in India, sum of parts is greater than whole. You will understand. I send you for some training to RSS School, Yuva Vidhya Kendra.'

And with that, and before Alice could protest, she was transported to a class-room full of children. The instructor told Alice that the aim of the school was to achieve what she called 'a wholistic perspective on education', whereby, all in one stroke, children would be enabled to improve their bodies, their minds, their grammar, and their culture. The means to this end was a course in reeling, writhing and rhythmetics, which consisted in conjugating the verb 'to take', to the accompaniment of much convoluted gesturing, pointing and gymnastics set to music. Alice heard a chorus of youthful voices, about a thousand in all, shouting: 'I TAKES, WE TAKES, YOU TAKES, HE TAKE, SHE TAKE, IT TAKE, THEY TAKES, EVERYBODY TAKE; I TAKES, WE TAKES, YOU TAKES, ...'

By and by, the words seemed to print themselves on little pamphlets, which (in the words of Mr Lewis Carroll himself) 'came flying down upon Alice; she gave a little scream, half of fright and half of anger, and tried to beat them off, and found herself lying on the bank, with her head in the lap of her sister, who was gently brushing away some dead leaves that had fluttered down from the trees upon her face.'

'Why, Alice dear, have you been dreaming in your sleep?' asked her sister gently.

'Yeth, tho I have', replied Alice.

'Why do you speak in that strange fashion, my dear?' asked her sister anxiously.

'Becauthe with a lithp, I ecthpect to be papoolar with the pippal', explained Alice.

'This is all very peculiar, Alice dear', her sister said in a worried voice. 'It's getting late; I'd like you to first go in to your tea and after that, you can tell me all about everything. Will you do that?'

'Yeth', said Alice, 'but for a conthiderathion.'

'And whatever on earth is that, my dear?' cried her sister.

'Theven per thent', said Alice with a thmirk.

## Learning to Swim
### (or)
## The Moral Currents of
## Current Morals

Several persons, for whose judgment I have the highest respect, while saying very kind things about this book, have added, that the great fault of it is, 'too much preaching'; but they hope I shall amend in this matter should I ever write again. Now this I most distinctly decline to do. Why, my whole object in writing at all, was to get the chance of preaching! When a man comes to my time of life and has his bread to make, and very little time to spare, is it likely that he will spend almost the whole of his yearly vacation in writing a story just to amuse people? I think not. At any rate, I wouldn't do so myself.

—Thomas Hughes
(Preface to the Sixth Edition of
*Tom Brown's Schooldays*, pp. 5–6, Ward,
Lock & Co. Limited, London and Melbourne)

# 10
## Moral and Political Economy
### *Hitopadesa* for the New Millennium*

Children, I'm sure you've all read stories from the *Panchatantra*. You can't possibly have forgotten those

* This piece originally appeared, under the same title, in *The Hindu*'s Sunday Magazine of 25 March 2001.

Immortally Illustrated Stories that appeared in lurid
comic books with the colour running out in a ghastly
sort of way from the pictures of foxes and tortoises
which you accepted, in your trustingly turnip-headed
way, as representations of foxes and tortoises. One
does not recover in a hurry from such traumatic
literary encounters. Well, then. It's on those stories
that the *Hitopadesa*, or Book of Good Counsel, an
ancient Sanskrit text, is based. Of late, the educators
in our country have begun to detect a foreign hand
in the *Hitopadesa* as it has been handed down to us.
How else, they argue, can one explain the complete
unsuitability to our times and culture of the morals
and maxims to be found in that text? In fact, the
Archaeological Survey of India has reported that a
whole clutch of palm leaves, constituting the text
of the *real Hitopadesa*, has recently been unearthed
at a site on the banks of the river Sarayu. These
findings suggest that ancient Indian civilization
had achieved an incredibly advanced level of
technological sophistication, on a par with that
of our own. This upholds the notion of a Cosmic
Wheel, or something on that order, in which things
appear, disappear, and reappear in cyclical epochs,
or *yugas*, or something like that (Look, if you have
all these questions, you really ought to be checking
them out with your grandmother. She just might

be able to bluff her way out of trouble). What this also proves is that the authentic *Hitopadesa* has been suppressed, and replaced by a subversive text—the work of barbaric invading hordes from Asia Minor—that has been handed down the centuries to us as the genuine article, as part of a millennial conspiracy to emasculate our true culture and enfeeble our racial potency. There is, in fact, a move afoot to pass an Act in Parliament whereby it will be statutorily binding, in the interests of reclaiming lost national pride, to identify the fake *Hitopadesa* by spelling it with an 'S' in front. Recently, the ICHR (Indian Council of Historical Regress) authorized an English language translation of the freshly unearthed (real) *Hitopadesa*, extracts from which are reproduced below. Read these, children, and discover the joy of having the cobwebs and confusion created by the fake forever blown away on the winds of a truly inspiring system of values that you should be able to recognize as your own, and identify with, and make the most of.

\*\*\*

## Extracts from the True Hitopadesa

The King addressed the great assemblage of wise men thus:

'O Sages and *pandits*, witness the misfortune, greater far than that of being burdened by a wife with a long tongue, that has befallen me. For I have a son, the Prince of this Realm, that is a wastrel and a dreamer. He has not the wherewithal to perform those kingly duties of statecraft, war, corruption, and corruption that must someday devolve upon his uncouth and misshapen shoulders, when I am called upon to shed these mortal coils and Yama claims me for his own. I know not under what stellar constellation of cosmic misfortune this offspring of mine was begotten. The worm of worry on his behalf eats my heart away, and keeps me from one productive kickback after another, one tyranny upon the citizenry after another. For he will not browse the internet; he speaks of truth and charity as if these were virtues; he reads *The Communist Manifesto*; he takes not the slightest effort to seek profitable intercourse with the underworld in the matter of arranging bat and ball contests; he speaks not of exacting tribute, but only of alleviating poverty; his mind is distracted forever by notions of old age pension, when he should occupy himself with apprenticeship to the art of fudging actuarial statistics; he believes in secularism and democracy. The catalogue is endless, but my time upon this planet is not. Will no one from among you, O men of learning and wisdom, take him in hand and instruct him in the art and craft of the political and moral sciences?'

Then it was that the great sage and scholar, Tantrabuddhisarman, venerated through the length and breadth of the country for his virtue and his erudition, rose and gave utterance, thus:

'Fear not, O King! He that has issued forth from your stock cannot for long stray from what has been ordained for him by his noble birth and lineage: in time, he must revert to his true nature. With good counsel and guidance, the Prince shall have his aberrations ironed out, and be set upon the path of success and attainment that have been destined for him. In six months, I shall instruct him in the art and craft of the political and moral sciences'.

Thereupon the King thanked Tantrabuddhisarman most humbly, and the Prince was entrusted to the seer's tutelage.

Tantrabuddhisarman well knew the merits of indoctrination through the medium of tales. Upon the Prince's eager acquiescence with the idea of learning from fables, Tantrabuddhisarman embarked upon—

## The First Story

Once, on the banks of the river Bhagirathi, there lived a snake called Seshanagananda. Not far from the snake's abode lived an old mongoose called Dantagaurava. Dantagaurava, calling out to Seshanagananda from his thicket, informed the latter in a piteous voice that old age was occasioning him untold dental trouble which interfered with his ingestion. Moved by the fate of the mongoose, Seshanagananda went over to his thicket, carrying with him a gift of false teeth. The mongoose pounced upon the snake, opened his mouth, and ate him up. This story upholds the moral that old age pensions are very bad. Dantagaurava had two friends, Nayamitra the dog, and Tavalaimitra the toad. To these latter two, he narrated—

## The Second Story

Once, on the banks of the river Gangotri, there lived a pigeon called Kabutarivathy. Despite the advice of all her friends, she steadfastly refused to learn computer software. But one day, when a storm began to brew, she found herself with no option but to order for an umbrella from a hardware store by email. Ignorant as she was of software, a virus called Vairasambhava emerged from the computer, opened his mouth, and ate up the pigeon. The story upholds the moral that it is a grave folly to turn your back on computers in this day and age when you should not only already be well on your way to Silicon Valley, but also respect your parents and your culture and say your ritual prayers three times a day, and be fully determined to continue to do so even after you have settled in San Jose. Vairasambhava had two friends—Hamsadhvani the swan and Margabandhu the leopard. To these latter two, he narrated:

## The Third Story

Once, on the banks of the river Godavari, there lived a fly called Makhimaitreyi. Makhimaitreyi had a friend, a horse called Kudremukhi. On a certain rainy day, Makhimaitreyi offered to tickle Kudremukhi's nose for him. Kudremukhi, who was willing to do anything for a laugh, fell in readily with the idea. Perched on his nose, Makhimaitreyi was most strategically placed. She opened her mouth, and ate up the horse. The moral of this story is that you mustn't trust anyone. The other moral is that you should always betray your friends. Another friend of Kudremukhi's, Bhagiravastraputra the tiger, was very relieved to be rid of his friend, and in gratitude for Makhimaitreyi's favour, he narrated to her—

## The Fourth Story

Once, on the banks of the river Brahmaputra, there lived a lion called Singhameswara, who had a rat slave called Chuhavardhini. Having been caught in the web of the prose of a crafty and subversive scholar called Karlamarkandaya, Singhameswara decided one day to give Chuhavardhini a fair wage.

Chuhavardhini, growing daily fatter on her fair wage, one morning caught Singhameswara taking a cat nap, whereupon she opened her mouth and ate up the lion. This story reveals the moral that communism, just like old age pensions, is very bad. Chuhavardhini then narrated, to her friend Gomukhi the cow:

### The Fifth Story

Once, on the banks of the river Kaveri, there lived a boar called Suvarnasundari. All the other creatures of the forest belonged to her community, save Hamsanandi the hedgehog. It was decided in a council meeting that Hamsanandi should be driven out of the forest, but Suvarnasundari held out, maintaining that communalism had no place in a secular and democratic society. She stuck to this position, despite the warnings of her friends. One day, Hamsanandi came up to Suvarnasundari and asked her if she believed Hamsanandi had a right to the beliefs enjoined on him by his community. When Suvarnasundari answered in the affirmative, Hamsanandi informed her that the doctrine of his community instructed him to eat boars. Saying this, he opened his mouth and ate up Suvarnasundari. From this story, we learn the moral that pseudo-secularism, minorityism, and false democracy are bad.

Within six months, the Prince of the Realm had been thoroughly instructed by Tantrabuddhisarman in the art and craft of the political and moral sciences, and he attained to a high degree of perfection in the onerous task of preparing to assume the King's mantle whenever the time for that should come.

# 11

## Law and Society

### Endgame*

(A Story for Children on the Dangers of Fuzzy Thinking)

This terrible tale warns of what could happen to you if you thought fuzzily. It goes as follows.

* This piece originally appeared, under the same title, in *The Hindu*'s Sunday Magazine of 1 October 2000.

It all began when the government decided it was time to do something about the dreadful state of Indian cricket. As to why it was dreadful, they had no doubts: If nothing good had come of the wretched thing, it must be because the rules of cricket hadn't served the nation well. The government, therefore, decided to subject the rules of cricket to a review. To this end, a review committee was constituted, with its own terms of reference, tenure, secretarial staff, and travel-cum-daily allowance. Each of these was indefinitely stretchable, and all of them were indefinitely stretched. The committee consisted of this and that member, and was chaired by a former Chief Justice of the Apex Court (which is what journalists always call the Supreme Court, just as they also always call elephants pachyderms). The CJ was a wise and humble man who had once scored one run (by way of a [miscredited] leg bye) in a very democratic cricket match between judges and women stenographers, before he was bowled a fourth time and the umpire (the CJ's private secretary) couldn't possibly call *yet another* no-ball.

As might be expected, the government's decision to call for a review evoked a storm of muddle-headed protest. (The supremo of one political party called for a CBI enquiry.) Academics, in particular, proved to be very difficult; and there was one Fuzzy Thinker who outdid the rest. This Fuzzy Thinker had both heard Granville Austin on the Indian Constitution, and read every single article published in a British journal of philosophy called *Analysis*. Accordingly, he maintained, loudly, that if there was to be any review, which he didn't see any need for, it should be very very specific, and very very public. Very specifically and publically, he called for a recognition of the conflict between intuitionism and legalism, something he had picked up on a beery afternoon from a reading of *Analysis*, which contained an article called 'The Umpire's Dilemma', written by a philosopher, also on a beery afternoon, in the mid-eighties.* The philosophical problem presented was the following one: The ball hits the batsman either on the pad or the bat before it lands in the wicketkeeper's gloves. The batsman's legs are plumb in front of the stumps. The umpire hears a sound but can't tell whether it's the bat or the pad. If it's the pad, the batsman ought to be given out lbw; if the bat, caught behind. Either way, he's out. But the rules require also that the batsman deserves the benefit of the doubt, and there's no provision in the rules stipulating a category of dismissals which goes: 'out leg before *or* caught'. If the umpire raises his finger, it's a case of Legalism; if he doesn't, it's a case of Intuitionism. What should he do?

* Colin Radford, 1985, 'The Umpire's Dilemma', *Analysis*, 45(2): 109–11.

The committee and the government were not impressed by any of this fuzzy thinking. Instead, by taking a broad-based, deep, general, and narrow view of things, they decided that the rules of cricket needed to be amended in two fundamental respects. First, any member of the other community could stake a claim for a place in the national eleven only if he surrendered his ration card and passport, which would be restored to him solely on condition that when he retired or was hanged (whichever happened later), he would have scored a century and taken at least five wickets in each innings he played, as proof of the absence of anti-national sentiment. Second, white flannels would be replaced by khaki shorts and saffron tunics. The two amendments were inspired, respectively, by the desire for a uniform civil code and a civil uniform code.

These amendments had the following consequences: First, India was expelled from membership to the ICC. Second, India won the World Cup in 2004. (The only World Cup event recognized by the Government of India was the two-nation tournament played by India and Nepal. In the 2004 final, India scored 1000 For No Loss in its allotted fifty overs, and won the match by default when Nepal, throwing a sulk, refused to bat.) Third, Ramachandra Guha's twenty-third book on Indian cricket was withdrawn from the Oxford University Press by the Indian Council of Sports, Culture and National Pride.

You're probably wondering what's so terrible about this tale. Here's the terrible part. The Fuzzy Thinker was frontally lobotomized to prevent fuzzy thinking and thereby to promote the interests of national security. I'm sure *you* wouldn't want a frontal lobotomy. If you don't, don't think fuzzily. The safest way to that end is not to think at all. So here's the moral of this truly true story: Children, be sure to distribute all your waking hours between drinking Koka (or, indifferently, Sepsis) Kola, watching *Ramayan* on television, and learning computer software. There won't be any need for the awful eventuality of a lobotomy.

# 12 Poverty

## Tiger's Tale (or) The Poor Men of Hindostan*

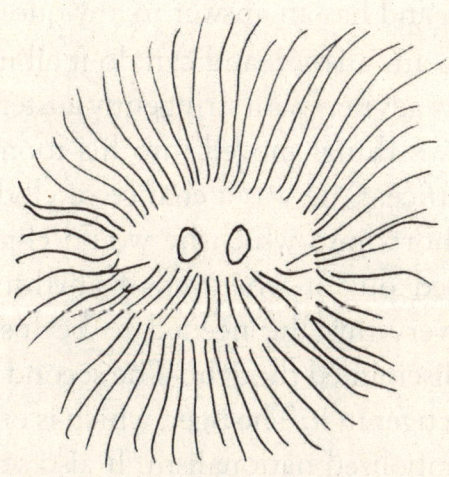

The Family was thoroughly overhauled to meet the challenges ahead, and this meant a change

* This piece originally appeared, under the same title, in *The Hindu*'s Sunday Magazine of 29 October 2000.

of leadership as well. The leader of the new look organization, the Revamped Self-Serving Sect, called a press conference immediately upon assumption of leadership, to declare that the sect had no intention of pressuring the government in any way, even though many members of the government were cousin sisters or co-brothers within the Family. After sending the journalists home the leader called the Prime Minister to tell him to appoint a Family Theoretician as Chief Economic Adviser to the government. A Family Theoretician is a person who knows everything about everything, and has an answer to any question and a question to any answer, and can do it all in Sanskrit.

The new adviser was a stringently austere man. He had only two things moved into his room when he assumed office. One was a change of clothes—a pair of khaki shorts into which he would climb (having first climbed out of whatever, if anything, he was wearing) every time he needed to be inspired into hard and disciplined thought. The second was a tiger cage with a tiger in it. The tiger, which is our national animal, symbolized nationalism. It also served other purposes, as we shall see.

The adviser called a meeting of experts to discuss poverty in the country. One fuzzy thinker, being an economist, said that the latest National Sample Survey data suggested an increase in the proportion of the population in poverty. 'Nonsense!' shrieked the adviser. 'How dare you base your conclusions on a thin sample? You're for the high jump.'

A second fuzzy thinker, who had a degree in literature and attended these meetings only for the lunch, attempted to introduce some levity into the proceedings by saying: 'Yon sample has a lean and hungry look. I like to have fat samples about me.'

'Shakespeare?' screamed the adviser. 'Are you aware that Shakespeare is *ultra vires* under the revised Constitution? The only classical allusions allowed are to Goswami Tulsidas. You're for the high jump, too.'

A third fuzzy thinker, also an economist, was a slow and plodding type who liked to begin from the beginning and get down to fundamentals. 'In measuring poverty', he said, 'it's useful to go about things systematically. A poverty measure is a function which effects a mapping from the non-negative orthant of n-dimensional Euclidean space to one-dimensional Euclidean space. We shall allow E to stand for the latter__'

Here he was interrupted by a howl of rage from the adviser. 'What you call Euclidean space is in fact Arya Bhatta space', he said, with every evidence of uncontrollable fury. 'This is a Western conspiracy. All the propositions of Euclid are actually due to Arya Bhatta; the rest are due to Bhaskara-I, and the remaining ones to Bhaskara-II. You, too, are for the high jump.'

At this point, another expert tried to ingratiate himself with the adviser. 'Imagine', he said, 'letting E stand for Euclidean space when we all know, and as my five-year-old daughter always informs me her Miss has told her so, that E stands for egg!'

Unfortunately, the ploy backfired. 'Egg?' screamed the adviser. 'Egg? Do I need to inform you that under the revised Constitution non-vegetarianism is banned? E for egg indeed! It's clear your daughter goes to a mission school. You're for the high jump, and so is your daughter's Miss. Now let me think.'

In the interests of thought, the adviser had to get out of his clothes in order to get into his khaki shorts. (One expert swooned at the sight.) (Another developed hiccups.) (A third had the fits.) In his thinking pants, the adviser thought ferociously and disciplinedly. Suddenly his brow cleared and a beatific smile suffused his face. 'I have', he said, 'got it. Using complex analysis and drawing liberally on Vedic mathematics, it has now become clear to me that the proportion of the population in poverty is precisely equal to the square root of minus twenty-three point four zero per cent.' Apparently struck by an association of ideas, he asked the Finance Secretary, who happened to be present, if he had remembered to arrange for the number zero and the decimal system to be patented. Since he hadn't, the adviser assured him that he too was for the high jump.

Quaking in his boots, an expert asked if the square root of a negative number wasn't an imaginary number. 'Precisely', replied the adviser coyly. 'It's my symbolic way of pointing out that poverty is an imaginary problem. There are no poor people in this country. Of course, not everybody is rich, and I'm thinking mainly of the traders.' Accordingly, all commodities in the public distribution system were priced, for those above the poverty line, at the economic cost of procurement, which being higher than the market price drove the entire population to the open market (there being no officially recognized poor person in the economy), which made things a little easier all round for the traders, the non-rich things.

The meeting was dismissed. Those who were for the high jump—five experts in all—were thrown into the tiger cage. I won't dwell on the messy details of what followed: I'm sure I can leave that up to your imagination. Why burden the little heads of my soft-hearted readers (or at any rate the soft heads of the little-hearted brutes) with painful specificities? I shall certainly not be explicit on all the crunching and munching, slurping and gloshing that happened, the splayed bones and the dribbling juices. No, no. Nor on all the pools and pools that accumulated. Suffice to say it was an exceptionally good day for the tiger, whose luck had certainly changed under the new dispensation. In a complete reversal of earlier policies of feeding minorityism, this government fed the minorities (to the tiger, that is). The tiger had also developed quite a distinguished taste for fuzzy thinkers, historians in particular.

Children, there are so many morals to be learnt from this tale that I scarcely know where to begin. Here's an abbreviated list of don'ts and don'ts. Don't use thin samples. Don't read Shakespeare. Don't learn Euclid. Don't go to mission schools. Don't worry about poverty. If you do, remember old Mister Tiger is waiting for you. You could be for the high jump.

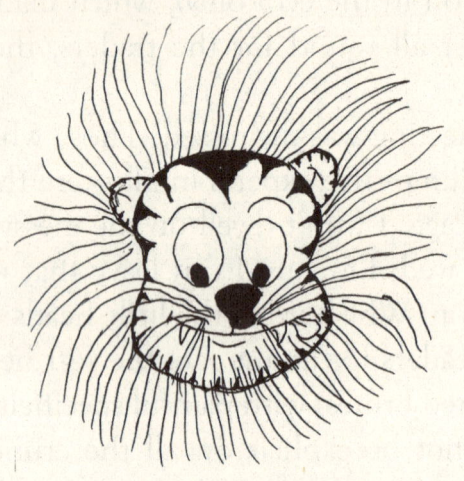

## Heroes of Our Times

If we sit, chin in hand, looking into the past and the present, we can see the torch-bearers. The long race of those who have borne and still carry the torches, passing them on from hand to hand, runs before us.

—Basil Mathews, M.A.
('The Relay Race',
in *The Race of Heroes*, p. 18,
S.W. Partridge & Co. Ltd., London)

# 13

## Law and Economics

## Contempt of Court

*High Court of Judicature versus*
The Indian Oppress

This piece is for the budding young lawyers among my readers—those idealistic young creatures with the gift for cramming hard legal words like 'milard' and 'de facto' which is required to secure the ends of truth, justice, and a decent standard of living. I shall certainly apply for assistance to one of them, in the years to come, when I am accused of plagiarizing A.P. Herbert, 'Beachcomber', and Tom Sharpe.

***

The High Court of _____ today witnessed remarkable scenes of drama, sensation, pity, and terror during the first (and last) hearing of a contempt proceeding, initiated *suo motu* by the Chief Justice, against the editor of the national daily, *The Indian Oppress*, for publishing, with documentary and photographic evidence, a story alleging that the Chief Justice had accepted and salted away a hefty bribe toward dismissing a case of corruption brought against the Chief Minister of the state by the previous government. The defendant was dragged into court in chains, to the accompaniment of whistles, catcalls, film songs, and the sound of breaking soda-water bottles from the spectators, in an even-handedly bipartisan display of sympathy and antipathy, at which point the court was called to order and the Chief Justice made his opening remarks.

'Having regard to the facts of the case, and whereas and hereunto said facts will be dismissed out of court, it will be the mandated brief of this court, in the interests of truth, impartiality and the summary dispensation of justice (Justice Brijbhushan Nyayadhikari: *Ex-kabbadi Reserve Players' National Federation vs. Union of India*), and with due deference to the *status quo ante* and the *status ex post facto*, to asseverate, *pari passu, mutatis mutandis, inter se*, and *in statu pupillari*, that, notwithstanding anything that may be laid down in the Constitution of India, the law will take its own course, in witness whereof it is my bounden duty, obligation and onus to now pass sentence on the defendant, as follows: _____ '

*Mr Sankaralinga Sambasiva Iyer (Senior Advocate and Counsel for Defence)*: 'With great respect, milard, if I may make so bold as to point out, milard, the case, milard, has not been heard, milard.'

*Chief Justice*: 'Counsel, you are an execrable louse, a loathsome lizard on the wall, and a piece of contaminated bird's dropping.'

*Defence Counsel*: 'All three, milard? Surely His Lardship's awesome intellect will perceive the improbability of being, milard, at one and the same time, milard, a louse, a lizard, *and* a piece of bird's dropping?'

*Chief Justice*: 'Have a care, sir! You are down there, and I am up here. It is at your own peril that you tangle, given your pathetic forensic ability, with the jurisprudential wisdom and expertise of a high legal eminence such as it would be a blow to my own proper modesty and humility to cite as an example— nay, I may say—as an exemplar!'

*Defence Counsel*: 'I hasten to assure you, milard, that it was never my intention to call into question the veracity of the fact that His Lardship is fairly eminent—'

*Chief Justice*: '*Fairly* eminent?'

*Defence Counsel*: 'That is to say, milard, it was my desire to articulate the view—in which I was frustrated, milard, by an inadvertent slip of the tongue, milard, arising, milard, from a transposition of the originally intended order of succession of the words, milard— that His Lardship is eminently fair, milard.'

*Chief Justice*: 'And?'

*Defence Counsel*: 'And very religious and spiritual, milard, and a dam-fine good-looker, if I may say so, milard.'

*Chief Justice*: 'You may yet have a future in the bar, sir, though it is salutary for you to be advised that you came dangerously close to inviting a charge of contumacious speech, which might then have necessitated my arraigning you along with your client, thus making it, appropriately, in these days of electronic appliances, a case of two in one.' (The Chief Justice signaled with a heart-chilling grimace that he had condescended to be humorous, and his remarks were greeted with titters of sycophantic laughter from the coterie's corner.)

*Defence Counsel*: 'His Lardship is unspeakably generous, and inexpressibly magnanimous. Sustained ratiocination in a calmer mood of mellow humility convinces me that His Lardship has let me too easily off the hook. I insist, milard, that His Lardship should visit violent corporal punishment with a cane or some similar appurtenance upon my humble nether quarters, milard.' Whereupon Counsel for Defence suddenly pulled down his trousers, bent over, and exposed his humble nether quarters, for, so to speak, His Lardship's information and appropriate action. Sixteen schoolgirls, in a high pitch of sexual hysteria, had to be thrown out of the court.

When order was restored, the Chief Justice resumed: 'This court has already been detained far too long by the wretched inanities of Defence Counsel. If that miserable bungler has nothing sensible to offer by way of defence, I should like to pronounce sentence against his client's colossal effrontery in pursuing the belief that he is free to offend the awful majesty of this court by telling the truth about the actions of the court's agents. This is a matter of law, not morality. Our Justices can—and, given my own proclivities in the matter I would go so far as to suggest that they should—be as corrupt and venal and vicious as they please. The more corrupt and venal and vicious they are, the more guilty of contempt of court one becomes by saying so. Defendant deserves to be shot, hanged, drawn and quartered, and to have his remains danced upon by me. Accordingly, I am disposed to pronounce the extreme sentence _____ '

*Defence Counsel:* 'Milard, milard, my client confesses his crime, and he repents. As a purely token gesture of penitence, you do understand, milard, do you not?— as a purely token and symbolic gesture, milard, my client wishes to impress upon His Lardship his true remorse, in evidence whereof, milard, I would invite His Lardship's attention to these three suitcases, each suitcase containing a bagatelle, milard, a wholly insubstantial gesture, the object being that His Lardship may view this as an offering at His Lardship's feet, and see His Lardship's way to an exoneration, milard, on the understanding, of course, that none of this shall be reported in the Press, milard _____ '

*Chief Justice:* 'Ah! This somewhat alters the complexion of the case. Defendant may be taken into custody and released after the cash has been counted

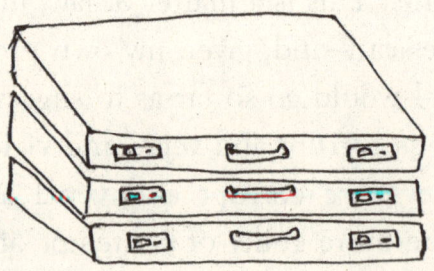

and found to be in proper order. Next time round, there can be no easy presumption as to the court's leniency. Case dismissed!'

# 14 Inflation

## The Price of Food*

This one, children, is for the future economists among you, who will do profit-maximizing political economy by working for the United States government from the Indian Planning Commission

* With acknowledgements to P.G. Wodehouse's *Augustus Fink-Nottle*.

after successful careers in the World Bank and the IMF.

***

$P$resident George W. Lush helped himself to a mighty big swig of bourbon, neat, and followed that up with another mighty big swig. He felt a little better. He then helped himself to a mighty big swig of bourbon, neat, and followed that up with another mighty big swig. He felt a deal better. He drew his sleeve across his lips, and squared his broad, manly shoulders. He narrowed his small, manly eyes, and surveyed the press folk of Poisonville.

'Boys, Girls, Ladies, Gemmen', said President George W. Lush, 'What, you ask, is the newest excuse for the war on terror? Lemme tell you. Dick Cheney has written a secret dossier for the CIA which warns that Saddam is momently returning from the Undead to lead a naxis of evil _____'

The President was gently interrupted and told that the question was on the price of food, not the war on terror.

George W. Lush, taking time off only for a mighty big swig of bourbon, broke out into immoderate laughter. Wiping his eyes and choking for breath, he gasped: 'Lemme tell you sump'n. What's the difference between (a) appreciating Condy and (b) what the Chinks are doing to food?'

In the silence that followed, the President, struggling with internal quakes of laughter, eventually managed to answer his own question: '(a) is Praising the Rice, and (b) is Raising the Price.' It took some time for Mrs Lush to emerge from the convulsions of hysterics that had seized her. When she had done so, the President swigged some more neat bourbon, smirked knowingly, giggled, and then doubled up, before resuming. 'Which reminds me of another one: What's the difference between a counterfeit dollar and a thin dame? This one's a bit risky. Counterfeit dollar's a phony buck, while thin dame's a _____'

A presidential aide reached out wildly for the President, grabbed his sleeve, and moaned desperately into his ear: 'Mr President sir, please sir, this is a press conference you are addressing, not a bunch of kids in a classroom'. The President viewed his aide with suspicion, considered the intelligence he had just received, and appeared to reluctantly agree that it made sense. 'Oh?' he said sullenly. 'OK, so tell 'em to get on with it. If this is a press conference, tell 'em to ask me questions. Gimme questions or gimme bourbon. Or better, both. Or best, just the bourbon.'

The President restored himself, while the aide anxiously reminded him of the query on the rise of food prices.

President Lush was impatient. 'But that question has already been answered by Condy. It's just like she said. It's a simple matter of demand and supply. What happens is that when demand goes down, price goes up'. Here the President's aide had another anguished whispering session with the President. 'Oh', said the President. 'John tells me it's the other way round. Or whatever. What? Oh. John tells me he's Tom, not John. Or whatever. But the point is, it's like Condy said. The Chinks and the Red Injuns have been growing at 10 per cent, and when you're growing at 10 per cent, you get fat, and eat more, and that pushes up the price of food. Demand and supply, like I said. What's it *now*, John? So all right, it's not the Red Injuns, it's the regular Injuns, the black, or brown ones, like that darky sitting right there, on the fourth row, third from the left. It's the principle of the thing that matters, not whether you're red or black or brown, as long as you're not white, and it's understood that biofuel and us have nothing to do with the rise in food price. Where's the darned bourbon? Any other question?'

A journalist drew the President's attention to the view that the per capita consumption of food by Poisonvillains was some five times that of Indians, so if the President's logic was right, all it would take to bring down food prices, obesity, *and* coronaries, in one stroke, was for Poisonvillains to go on a mild diet.

President George W. Lush bristled. 'What d'you mean per capita? Think I don't know what per capita is? Well, lemme tell you. Washington, D.C., that's what per capita is, just like London's the per capita of England and Rome's the per capita of Spain. And anyway, what d'you mean, five times? That's a filthy rumor. It's a damned lie and a rotten scandal, put out by a naxis of evil led by Osama bin Laden and Saddam, back from the Undead. You are for us or against us. You are for us or for a naxis of evil.'

What practical measures, a journalist wished to know, would the President propose in order to bring down food prices?

'It's a matter of demilinating menand. Medinitating lemand. That is to say, eliminating demand', said the President. 'The Injuns and the Chinks are growing at 10 per cent, and getting fat, and eating too much under the influence of a naxis of evil led by Osama bin Laden and Saddam, back from the Undead. It's time to cut the Injuns and the Chinks down to size. What we need is support. Those were the days, before this jerk Brown took charge. YO BLAIR, WHERE ARE YOU?'

The President became sentimental, and blew his nose, and wiped his eyes, before proceeding manfully. 'Never mind. If we have to go it alone, we'll go it alone. I've been talking to God, and He's been talking right back. I've got it all worked out, between us. We'll have to declare war on the Injuns and the Chinks. Shaw', said the President, slurring a bit, and then clarified: 'Shock-and-Awe. The Injuns and the Chinks are getting to become too many and too prosperous on account they're growing at ten per cent and getting fat and pushing up the price of food. So all we need to do is spread some death and poverty around. Shaw, like I said. Some nice depleted uranium should do the job. That will be Poisonville's way of defending freedom and democracy and the price of food.'

'The bourbon's on the house.'

\*\*\*

Within hours of the press conference, Hillary Clinton, ahead of the remaining primaries, promised the people of Poisonville that if she was elected, she would attack not only Iran but also India and China.

# 15

## International Relations

## High Loon
### (or)
## The War on Terror

(As it might have been written, in collaboration, by Stephen Leacock and Zane Gray)

Sheriff George W. Lush helped himself to a mighty big swig of bourbon, neat, and followed that up with another mighty big swig. He felt a little better. He then helped himself to a mighty big swig of bourbon, neat, and followed that up with another mighty big swig. He felt a deal better. He drew his sleeve across his lips, and squared his broad, manly shoulders. He narrowed his small, manly eyes, and surveyed the townsfolk of Poisonville. The Poisonville folk were a God-fearing, peace-loving lot, who went about their daily business, killing only for gold or fun, whipping their slavies only for their own good, shooting the odd Injun down only to rid the country of vermin, and lynching the odd crook only because he wasn't the right color. These good people had had it up to here with that no-good bandit Osmo Ben Ladd—Ossy the Lad he called himself—and they had gathered together in the town square, in front of the bar, to hear the Sheriff talk tough. In order to talk good, the Sheriff, like I said, first had to square his broad, manly shoulders, and narrow his small, manly eyes. The townsfolk of Poisonville greeted him with loud cheers, and sang the Poisonville anthem. The Sheriff was moved to tears. He wiped his eyes, took a mighty big swig of bourbon, felt better, wiped his lips, placed his hand on his heart, and spoke:

'Ah'm agoanter hunnim daoun.'

The townsfolk of Poisonville rent the air with loud cheers.

'Is y'all agoanter help me?' asked the Sheriff.

The townsfolk of Poisonville rent the air with louder cheers.

'Ah'm agoanter chase him from place to place, till he ain't got no place to go, an' no place to hide. Ah'm agoanter flush him out. I wannim—daid or alive. There's a bounty of a million dollars on his lousy haid.'

The townsfolk of Poisonville rent the air with the loudest cheers yet.

'Before Ah does that', said the Sheriff, narrowing his eyes so you could hardly see them (and he could hardly see out of them), 'Ah'm agoanter shoot lots of people, on account they's all friends of Ossy the Lad. Who're these low-life scum? yew ask. They's anybody that don't go along with me, and the rest of us folks from Poisonville.'

'Get 'em! Shoot 'em! Burn 'em! Hang 'em high!' cried the good people of the town. 'God bless Poisonville!'

'The rat is hidin' out in Miss Packy Stan's salon,' said the Sheriff, 'so first, Ah'm agoanter have to tell her to give him up.'

The Sheriff strode up to Packy Stan's salon. In his courtly, old-fashioned way, and because he had been brought up on family values, George W. Lush took off his hat to the lady of ill repute. (A pair of cruel eyes gave the Sheriff the once-over from behind a chest of drawers.) The Sheriff told Packy that he wasn't there to make any deals, and Packy promised to hand over Ossy the Lad if he should wind up at her salon, provided the Sheriff restored to her all the licenses he had cancelled all those years ago, and got the Town Bank to wipe out all her debts and lend her enough lucre to help her set up a dozen more salons. The Sheriff brought his lips together in a thin, manly line, and inclined his manly head. 'Sho' do 'ppreciate yo' help, ma'am,' he said, and allowed himself a brief, shy, rugged smile, as Packy kissed him full on his manly lips, while she also rifled his manly pocket.

George W. Lush strode out of the salon into the heat and dust and awful silence of the high noon. The sun was at its zenith, and there wasn't a shadow you could see. With measured strides, the Sheriff walked sixty paces into the center of town, under the hushed and watchful gaze of the people of Poisonville.

'C'mon out, yew yaller dog!' shouted the Sheriff, in his manly voice. There was no sign of Ossy the Lad.

'This is yer last chance, vermin!' rasped the Sheriff. There was still no sign of Ossy the Lad.

'Reach fer it, yew cowerin' coyote!' There was still no sign of Ossy the Lad.

'This town ain't big enough fer the two of us!' There was still no sign of Ossy the Lad.

'Eat lead, scum!' And, as there was still no sign of Ossy the Lad, Sheriff Lush whipped out his revolver madly, and fired madly off in all directions.

In the fetid heat of the high noon, Sheriff George W. Lush shot himself in the foot. And because his foot was always in his mouth, well—you can figure out for yourselves the sad and messy end.

No, you can't! Sheriff Lush was indestructible! Sprawled though he was on the ground, he still managed to square his shoulders and narrow his eyes and smile his crooked, if now bloodied, smile, as, reaching for his bourbon, he grated: 'Aw, shit. I ain't done with the axis of evil yet. I'll still get 'im.'

And the generous folk of Poisonville cheered loudly and sang the Poisonville anthem and re-elected Sheriff George W. Lush to another term.

# VERSE FOLLIES
## The Lyrical Sides to
## Economy and Society

Some thinkers, like Samuel Johnson, fail to become philosophers because cheerfulness keeps obtruding. Some economists, on the other hand, become versifiers because depression keeps obtruding. After all, one needs some relief from maximizing utility: If you spent all your life mucking about with a bordered Hessian matrix, you could quite easily wind up developing a tic or performing St Vitus' Dance or composing limericks. Hence the ensuing rhymes ... which I shall risk calling Econometrical Scales—easily the sort of thing that can attract paperweights aimed at the perpetrator's head.

... peoms which creep in from time to
time ...

—Nigel Molesworth
(in Geoffrey Willians'
*How To Be Topp*)

# 16

## An Ode on Poverty
### The Saga of World Poverty*

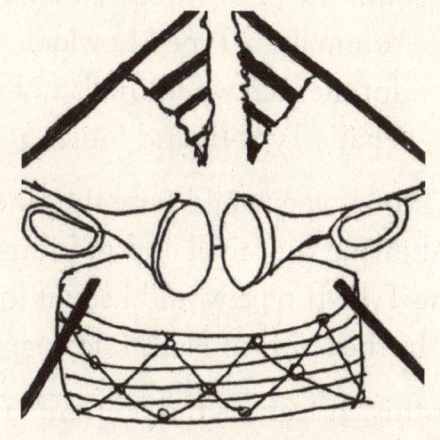

If crisp, or exact, logic is sound,
Of this we can be sure:
There're only two kinds of folks around—
The Rich, and then, the Poor.

* This verse was published as 'An Ode on Poverty: The Saga of World Poverty', *Challenge: The Magazine of Economic Affairs*, 52(4): 106-8, July/August, 2009. Copyright © 2009 by M.E. Sharpe, Inc. Reprinted here by permission.

But who is who, and which is which?
That's the riddle in fine.
What queers the blasted ruddy pitch
Is drawing the Poverty Line.

You can draw it right or draw it wrong,
Or up, or down, or middling;
You can draw it short or draw it long,
Or straight, or somewhat diddling.

If you count me poor when I'm really not,
You make a Type-I howler;
If you count me rich when that's not my lot,
That's Type-II, and fouler.

A Type-I type would raise the floor,
Abjuring the small and piddling;
The Type-II type would keep it low,
In the spirit of Nero fiddling:

Or this, at least, is the point of view
In every current debate
Which accounts for all the cry and hue
On the Global Poverty Rate.

In fits and starts, and now and then,
The bank gives estimates
(From Martin Rave and Show-How Chen)
On global headcount rates.

A few, more loyal than the king,
Have performed some startling tricks
Designed to show it's a simple thing
To fix the statistics—

In such a way as to eliminate,
And secure the stultification,
Of any serious headcount rate—
Through scalar multiplication.

One or two have sat on the fence,
Or given that impression;
What possibly makes more solid sense
Is praise through faint damnation.

We arrive at last at the World Bank's bogey—
You should see the attack they are mounting:
Sun-joy Red and Thomas Fogey—
They teach the World Bank counting.

'How not to count the poor', they say,
'Is how the Bank does count them':
Well-mannered people would shun this way
Of visiting needless mayhem.

Fixing the norm at a dollar a day
Is something they denigrate:
'How', they ask, 'can you possibly say:
"This way to calibrate"?

'Does it make meaning, conceptual sense?—
Apart from the simple fact
That you can't live on a hundred cents—
Pardon the lack of tact.'

Then there is strife on the PPP rate,
With which rupees are changed into dollars:
The bank loves this, which others hate—
This is often the way with scholars.

One cannot avoid the taking of sides
In a quarrel such as this.
(It's useful to have the thickest of hides
In case of a boo or hiss.)

For myself, I feel the time
Has come for two sensible acts:
For me to end this tiresome rhyme,
And for the bank to face up to the facts.

# 17 Clerihews in Merry Hues

## An A to Z of the Lives and Times of Economists in Jolly Rhymes*

clerihew

n.

A humorous verse, usually consisting of two unmatched rhyming couplets, about a person whose name generally serves as one of the rhymes.

* This originally appeared in the *Royal Economic Society Newsletter*, Issue 146: 17–18, July–September, 2009.

[After Edmund Clerihew Bentley (1875–1956), British writer.]

—*The American Heritage Dictionary of the English Language*

— • —

'The art of Biography
Is different from Geography.
Geography is about Maps,
But Biography is about Chaps.'

—Edmund Clerihew Bentley

— • —

The selection of the twenty-six economists featured here may well be eccentric. This should encourage other scholars to come up with their own twenty-six clerihews apiece. If five economists undertook this task, we should have on hand a slim and elegant volume of one hundred and thirty verses. I offer this suggestion at no cost to the Royal Economic Society, although, of course, I shouldn't complain if they offered, in exchange, to publish one or two (or three) of my articles in *Economic Journal* (without charging a submission fee, I hope it goes without saying).

A

Kenneth Joseph **Arrow**,
Compared to Mia Farrow,
In oomph is deficient.
But his equilibrium is efficient.

— • —

B

**Bentham**, of Utilitarian fame,
Swore up and down by this claim:
You are cracked, or at least tight,
To respect a natural right.

— • —

C

Says Ronald Harry **Coase**
(In very simple prose):
Define the rights of property
And be rid of externality.

— • —

D

Monsieur Gerard **Debreu**
Wrote neither Greek nor Hebrew.
Still it's hard to argue
With his *Theory of Value*.

— • —

*E*

Francis Ysidro **Edgeworth**
Is known from Rio to Fort Worth
For the *brio* and swerve
Of his contract curve.

— • —

*F*

To Professor Milton **Friedman**
All things under the sun
Suggested the supply of money.
Dr Solow found this funny.

— • —

G

William Terence **Gorman**
Was not, I think, a Mormon.
He did tricks with a utility function
And got lost at Didcot Junction.

— • —

*H*

Trygve Magnus **Haavelmo**
Differed from Larry, Joe and Curly Mo
Whose talents were not statistical
But really rather slappy-stick-al.

— • —

## I

**Inada**, Ken-Ichi
One consults when itchy
To display one's deference
For non-cyclical preference.

— • —

## J

William Stanley **Jevons**
Didn't habitually gaze at the heavens,
Though his work on sun-spots
Could lead to such thoughts.

— • —

## K

John Maynard **Keynes**
Quite bursted with brains.
The rational outcome
Was more national income.

— • —

## L

Wassily **Leontief**
Was born in Munich, not Kiev.
Whenever he was able,
He drew a coefficients table.

— • —

M

For Thomas Robert **Malthus**
There's too many of us.
He feared humanity's fate
Is in its reproductive rate.

— • —

N

John Forbes **Nash**,
You should recognize in a flash,
Is the swellest of names
In the Theory of Games.

— • —

O

**Ohlin** said to Heckscher,
'You betcher I'm glad I metcher' –
A Wodehousean line
For this happy combine.

— • —

P

For Vilfredo Federico **Pareto**
It's true from Sicily to Soweto
That $x$ is socially the best
If it's best for me, and the rest.

— • —

## Q

Of Francois **Quesnay**
One can rightly say
That his Economic *Tableau*
Is something. *Parbleu!*

— • —

## R

**Robinson**, by whom I mean Joan,
For this taunt was very well known:
'How dare you measure capital
When you are neoclassical?!'

— • —

## S

Amartya Kumar **Sen**
Is a prince among men.
But he *will* sprain your brain
With a Theorem of Szpilrajn.

— • —

## T

The economics of **Tobin**
Is deep and very probing.
He did not care much
For monetarists and such.

— • —

## U

Hirofumi **Uzawa**,
Is admired from near and far.
A critic is one who hectors
His model of two sectors.

— • —

## V

Thorstein Bunde **Veblen**
Denounced conspicuous consumption.
He thought the leisure class
To be a pain in the _____.

— • —

## W

Marie-Esprit-Leon-**Walras**
Was an economist of the very first class.
That excess demands sum to zero
Is a law of this mathematical hero.

— • —

## X

No economists were called Xaliah,
Or Xerxes or Xantha or Xavier.
No matter what sex,
They are badly served by X.

— • —

## Y

Janet Louise **Yellen**
Is at Berkeley, not Mellon.
She thinks unemployment's sad,
But inflation less bad.

— • —

## Z

Arnold **Zellner**'s Ecotricks
Is largely Bayesian statistics.
To say what that means
Would be spilling the beans.

— • —

# 18
## Concavity

## The Pivotal Point
## (or)
## The Mathematical
## Economist's Anthem*

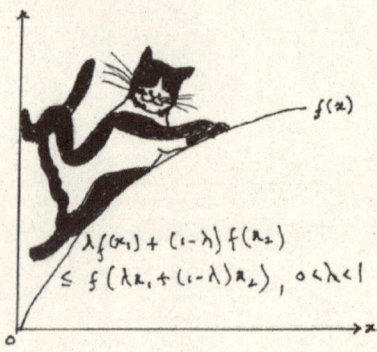

$$f(x)$$

$$\lambda f(x_1) + (1-\lambda) f(x_2)$$
$$\leq f(\lambda x_1 + (1-\lambda) x_2), \quad 0 < \lambda < 1$$

[This verse's rhyme and metre are, I believe, a recognizable plagiarism of T.S. Eliot's 'MaCavity:

* This originally appeared as one of two verses under the common title 'Verse and Worst: Two Poetic Excesses in Economics or, perhaps, Two Economic Excesses in Poetry', *The Heterodox Economics Newsletter* of 30 June 2010 (available at http://www.heterodoxnews.com/).

The Mystery Cat', which appears in his collection *Old Possum's Book of Practical Cats*. It points to the ubiquity of 'concavity' in mainstream economic theory, extolling its virtues, and underlining its indispensability for the heroic task of doing mathematical economics. It may be added that, if needs must, this anthem can also be sung—even tunefully, thanks to Andrew Lloyd Webber. (*Author's Note*)]

\*\*\*

Concavity's the pivotal point: it drives each Worldly Law –
It's the reason why indifference curves fill us all with awe.
Micro, macro, the lot of it, would be beyond repair,
And all of it a waste of time—*if concavity's not there!*

Concavity, concavity, there's nothing like concavity,
You need it here, you need it there, you need it for duality.
The dismal science is dismaller, quite stark and wholly bare,
Not worth a single, solitary dime—*if concavity's not there!*
No output curve that you can sketch, I dare and double dare,
Will the Law of Declining Returns fetch, *if concavity's not there!*

Concavity's a handsome thing, a very distinguished curve.
A concave utility function has a typically sloping swerve,
Without which, I fear, we cannot say much
About prospects, bets and such,
Nor say of a person that she's risk-averse
In accents brisk and terse.

Concavity, concavity, there's nothing like concavity—
You can't do without it when you measure inequality:
When you need something like the Gini, 'tis poorly you will fare
With a social welfare function in which *concavity's not there*!
With concave curves and convex sets and a result of Mangasarian,
You should be able to get somewhere with your intermediate Varian;
Failing which I rather fear you'll have to tear your hair—
Which is the lot of the economist for whom CONCAVITY'S NOT THERE!

# 19

## Alchoholic Disclaimer

### Being a Fragment of Verse Recently Discovered in the Ogden Nash Archives*

This verse is perhaps the only tragic poem written by the late great comic poet Ogden Nash, and it tells of

* This originally appeared as one of two verses under the common title 'Verse and Worst: Two Poetic Excesses in Economics or, perhaps, Two Economic Excesses in Poetry' in *The Hetrodox Economics Newsletter*, Issue 161 of 30 June 2010 (available at http://www.heterodoxnews.com/).

the profound sorrows that often come in the wake of
mistaken identities.

***

After wine and pickled mackerel,
One cannot always rightly tell
Which Nash is John
And which is Ron,
Or which is Ben
And which Ogden.
Of mixing up people in ways mistaken,
The chances, then, are nine on ten.
And so, at cocktail parties, oft,
Some one comes and whispers soft –
Some one in academia –
'John, I think I really deem ya
(Upon my mickled packerel)
To be Game Theory's greatest swell.'
'Upon your crippled caramel',
I tell Professor McNicknicholl
(Or whoever it is that has come along
And got it all completely wrong),
'I think you think I'm Nash the John,
You poor, misguided, sozzled don.
But John I'm not, who even when drowsy,
At math is hot, while myself am lousy.
No pedagogue is Nash the Og,
So get this through your 'holic fog:

He's not to be
Mis-thought as me:
*That* Nash
Doesh equilibrash,
While *thish* Nash
Doesh poetic mish-mash.
To tell us apart
Is no great art:
Just grasp this detail –
The Prize Nobel
Is for John,
In Econ;
And ought to be
– Holy Mockerel! –
For me
– In Doggerel.'

# 20
## Newspaper Verses 1
### Brahmin Kosher

*Mrs Thathachari [name altered] wants to give a suggestion. She feels that there are people of many different castes who will not eat food cooked by a person of another caste. So, can restaurants like Saravana Bhavan have special cooks of different castes who can provide food for people of the same caste, for e.g. Brahmin cooks who will cater for Brahmin customers only.*

—Rashmi Uday Singh's 'Good Food Line',
in *The Hindu* (Metroplus), c. AD 2000

\*\*\*

Old Thatha was so orthodox
He wore no shoes nor stylish socks,
Nor, indeed, designer jocks,
But only hand-washed loincloths.

One day the devil seized him good,
And made him lust for sinful food.
Old Thatha barged into the Taj
Like a captain leading a cavalry charge.

He gorged himself on meat and fish
And consumed each single fleshly dish
Listed on the a la carte:
Old Thatha ate with soul and heart.

And when he had eaten to his fill
The waiter slapped him with the bill:
What a wild and wondrous super bash!
Alas! Not backed up by cash.

Mrs Thatha now entered,
Wishing Thatha deep interr'd;
But when she saw him lone and 'fraid,
She rushed to him with wifely aid.

The waiter she fixed with a baleful look:
'What caste is he, your frightful cook?
'Not *Saama Vedi**, did you say?
'THEN NOT A PIE WILL THATHA PAY!'

---

* An A#1 high class brahmin, for the benefit of the ignorant
and unwashed.

# 21

## Newspaper Verses 2

## A Snake in the House*

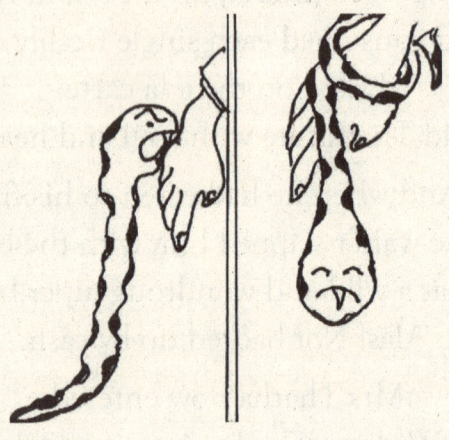

BHUBANESWAR: *A snake which strayed into the Orissa Assembly on Thursday was finally caught on Saturday morning.*

*Several members were still inside the Assembly when a watchman spotted the snake around 9 p.m., minutes*

---

* R. Padmanabhan shares responsibility for this, and is at least halfway implicated.

*after the House was adjourned, and immobilized it with a chair.*

*A snake expert, who was waiting outside the Assembly, was called in and he caught the reptile.*

*In the process, the snake bit the catcher and a Marshal of the House.*

*The Hindu: Sunday, July 26, 2009*

\*\*\*

In an Assembly full of slimy snakes, why should one more raise the stakes?

Because he is truly serpentine, while the rest are full of turpentine—

Or turpitude—of the moral kind that with certitude you are bound to find

In any gang of elected crooks infesting all the House's nooks,

And fearful lest their acts of fraud be punished by sundry acts of God

Like snakes that just may wander in to their den of vice and criminal sin.

To save their worthless wretched hides they circled the snake on all four sides,

And it became the House's daily feature to push and poke and prod the creature—

Whether cobra, rat or sand or krait we dare not ask nor speculate

Till *The Hindu*, after it has checked out thrice, is satisfied it tells no lies.

But a snake by any name, they said, is seldom without blame undead,

For a snake alive could poison your blood and nip your career in the bud,

And along with it corruption's fruit—those income streams of bribes and loot.

Eager to save their precious skin, and the futures of their kith and kin,

They tailed a dermatologist, and hailed a herpetologist,

And additional, and furthermore, they pushed a marshal to the fore:

Despite his being coy and cringing, they hollered 'hoy!' in timbres ringing,

And scrabbling, grabbing, scuffling, shoving, forced him forward, shrilly yielding,

To do his duty by god and nation, with a proper notion of his station.

The expert and the marshal both, having been commanded forth,

Upended a chair upon the snake, and dared thereafter to undertake—

Driven to it by carrot and stick—to grab him in one swooping pick.

The serpent was rightly pissed by this, so he opened his jaws and hissed a hiss,

And brought them down upon the pair, biting the duo fair and square.

What happened next *The Hindu* hid: upon the rest it brought down the lid:

For what followed now was a bit too dark for its gentle readers to view or hark:

The human poison was fatally dire, causing the snake to curl up, expire.

# FINIS

Ho fie lo egad and away for it is the BELL
and it tolleth for me cheers cheers cheers.

—Geoffrey Willans
('How To Be Topp', reprinted in
Alan Coren (ed.), *The Penguin
Book of Modern Humour*, p. 244,
Penguin Books Ltd., Middlesex, 1982)

# 22
## An Ending in Sweet Verse

Through timely tales of terrible truth,
And children more uncouth than couth,
I've told of sundry juvenile slimes
Who are shining mirrors of their times.

Through stories choice, and moral, too,
I've dealt with values false and true,
I've shown the ways of right and wrong,
To guide the little skunks along.

Children, learn your lessons well:
Always cheat, and cheat like hell.
Win by hook, or win by crook:
That's the moral of this book.

Hate your neighbour, do him in:
Exploit class and caste and kin;
Nothing's foul and all is fair
When you little care and nothing share.

If your grandpa messes up your hair,
Or elsewise is a bad nightmare,
Just chop him up in little bits
And feed the pieces to the kits.

Love your country, milk it dry
Before to $-land you fly;
And when you're settled overseas,
Save India from the OBCs.

Save it, too, from people who,
By cunning means, will threaten you,
And seal your poor and piteous fate
With an awesome fertility rate.

Meanwhile my dears, to help you grow
In ways to make your parents glow
With pride (while others fetch their pails),
I offer you these little tales.

Through ups and downs, and thick and thin,
Fight your way with cunning sin;
Of theft and fraud and crooked barter,
Learn your ropes from Atafata-ta.

And when to adulthood you've grown,
And understood the lessons I've sown,
You'll see what wondrous tales are these
That've helped you with your scams and sleaze.

The time has come to say goodbye,
And I should surely tell a lie
If I said I'm sad to bid farewell
To all you sordid ticks from hell.

# What the Critics Say of Economic Offences

## A Cross-section of Scholarly Opinion

*Review of Higher Education, Moral Rearmament, and Free Verse* (in collaboration with *Roget's Thesaurus*):
'... disgusting, nauseating, sickening, revolting, repulsive, loathsome, abhorrent... All of the verses rhyme ...'

\*\*\*

*Interjections: A Journal for Postcolonial Buddies*:
'Brer Rabbit an' de Cricket Match', by an Indian? ... Edward Said never had to theorize an oriental dis coarse ... What did I do to deserve it? ... to read it against the grain is to court strabismus, to read it any other way is to be imbricated in textual harassment ... the Mummy/Daddy binary opposition as an a/o/ccidental discursive displacement of gendered subjectivity is a failed effort at recovering the alterity

of the m/other, not to mention the anteriority of the grandm/other ... This work should be valorized, if at all, not for its *jouissance* but for its *nouissance* ...'

\*\*\*

*Review of Briefless Therapy:*
'... A remarkable work which highlights the paradox of ontology: How can anything so awful exist? ... of mixed therapeutic value: it both cures and engenders schizophrenia, in either case through the sheer force of bad taste ...'

\*\*\*

*Quarterly Journal of Freedom, Entitlement, Value, Welfare, Choice, Development, Measurement, Capability, and Utility:*
'... for the impact of adult literacy on capability expansion, see, among others [list of 168 references]. On the impact of children's literature on fertility reduction, see (*but only if there is no help for it*) the regrettably published monograph by S.S.: *Economic Offenses* ...'

\*\*\*

*Indian Journal of Tabular Economics* (reprinted in *Indian Review of Compulsory Regression Research*):
'... interregional variations are not considered ... the same holds for non-sampling errors ... otherwise very bad ...'

\*\*\*

# About the Author

S. SUBRAMANIAN is a professional Fuzzy Thinker, that is, he gets paid (though far from enough) to think fuzzily. He copes with this situation like all other fuzzy thinkers, namely, by adjusting marginal product to wage, or, in practical terms, by generating a mix of fuzz and thought which is overwhelmingly weighted in favour of the former. S.S. was born to blush unseen. He has only once consented to an interview, an occasion on which he spoke from behind a veil. He was very reticent about his publishing history, but upon being questioned closely, it emerged he had once published an essay titled `The Liberal Paradox with Fuzzy Preferences', and twenty-two years thereafter, another essay titled 'The Arrow Paradox with Fuzzy Preferences'. When asked what these were about, he proved to be very evasive until, in the face of relentless cross-examination, he eventually broke down, wept, and confessed that he did not have the slightest idea. In the matter of his non-professional writing, it appears that he is in possession of the manuscript of a trilogy titled *The Chronicles of Atafatata*, consisting of three works, namely and respectively:

1. *Ata's Almanack of Atavistic Attitudes*;
2. *Fata's Folio of Flatulent Fantasmagoria*; and
3. *Ta-ta's Text of Tantalizing Travesties*.

It is the author's considered opinion that Thomas Mann's tetralogy *Joseph and his Brethren* compares not unfavourably with his own trilogy. A somewhat less partisan view suggests that, should the light of day ever settle on these works, whether individually or in some omnibus edition, then they shall meet with the same fate which the present work deserves, which is to be flushed unseen.